# Graphic Design Processes

to Eleanor, Stephanie, Chris, and Sara—
the four unique women in my family . . .

*Kenneth J. Hiebert*

# Graphic Design Processes

**...u n i v e r s a l   t o   U n i q u e**

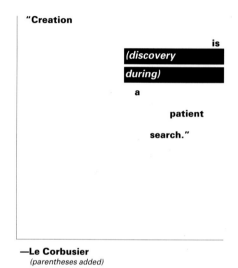

"Creation

is

*(discovery*

*during)*

a

patient

search."

—**Le Corbusier**
*(parentheses added)*

**VNR** Van Nostrand Reinhold
New York

**Design by Kenneth Hiebert
Printed in the United States of America**

**Van Nostrand Reinhold
115 Fifth Avenue
New York, New York    10003**

**Chapman and Hall
2–6 Boundary Row
London, SE1 8HN, England**

**Thomas Nelson Australia
102 Dodds Street
South Melbourne 3205
Victoria, Australia**

**Nelson Canada
1120 Birchmount Road
Scarborough, Ontario M1K 5G4, Canada**

16 15 14 13 12 11 10 9 8 7 6 5 4 3 2 1
**Library of Congress Cataloging-in-Publication Data**

Hiebert, Kenneth J.
Graphic design processes: universal to unique / Kenneth J. Hiebert
    p.   cm.
    Includes Index
    ISBN 0-442-00839-2

1. Graphic Arts—Technique.
2. Design.
3. Computer Graphics—Technique.
I. Title.

NC1000.H54   1991    741.6—dc20                          91–4384
                                                            CIP

The quotation on page 24, which serves as a key
to this book, as well as other quotations from
*Grammatical Man,* © 1982 by Jeremy Campbell,
are reprinted with permission of Simon &
Schuster. The excerpt on page 30 from *Invisible
Cities* by Italo Calvino, copyright © 1972 by
Giulio Einaudi editore s.p.a., English translation
copyright © 1974 by Harcourt Brace Jovanovich,
Inc., is reprinted by permission of Harcourt Brace
Jovanovitch. Please see page 203 for a complete
list of acknowledgments. The development of this
book was supported in part by a grant from the
National Endowment for the Arts, a Federal
agency.

# **C** o n t e n t s

**Projects**

## 1.

Space is the common denominator of a visual composition, the glue. In this project, strict formal limitations are accepted to emphasize the use of space as a dynamic field which contributes directly to the expression of the content.

## 2.

The alphabet is a logical and convenient base for sign-symbols. Participants in a summer session apply a catalog of letter variation options (morphology) to a set of three letters to develop a sign-symbol identity for the session itself. The letters CM–B derive from Carnegie Mellon (University) and Basel (Switzerland), the alternating host locations. In the expansion phase a poster motif is developed.

## 3.

Words can function as captions, labels, or integrated elements in relation to picture images. The focus here is the integration of words and images, a classic problem for the graphic designer. A program is explored for building a set of variations on a three-word text in combination with a separate set of photographic and video-graphic images of the cup.

## 4.

Texture and pattern are universally attractive aspects of visual form. A study trip to the Oaxaca Valley of Mexico provides the context for this project. Using a daily sketch routine and a combination of intentional and chance methods, impressions and place/time data are overlaid. Textures and patterns are derived from drawings, rubbings, and photographs. After returning home, the sketchbook images are processed into a more definite form. These forms stimulate probes into fresh combinations, suggesting new potential for graphic expression.

## 5.

Because of its emotional impact and because individual preferences are strong, color is a difficult subject to study objectively. In this project, a structure for understanding color interaction is described and relevant color terms are defined. Limiting color to a specific set (triad) establishes a base for an exploration of its basic qualities—hue, intensity, and lightness—and how they affect the interaction of color. Out of this exploration a unique color quality or resonance is progressively developed and applied to a series of posters.

## 6.

Creativity is characterized by the overlap or convergence of two otherwise unrelated ideas. This project is a catalyst to challenge students to find a way to overlay ideas for characterizing a profession or vocation on an analog clock face of their own design. Three working clocks are made: a study clock and two clocks with vocational connotations. The clocks are named and an appropriate, simple logo is designed. A package design completes the assignment.

## 7.

Graphic images presented over time is the subject of this project. A logotype designed for a museum is the basis. A morphology of changes in form and movement and a modular notational system for scoring animation sequences over time are developed. (Assembled sequences in color are available on a separately available computer disk.)

# **A**cknowledgments

I would like to acknowledge with deepest gratitude the persons who have contributed to the building of this book. First and foremost, my teacher, Armin Hofmann, who taught me more than any other to see and to think visually and to maintain a constant vigil against the dilution and waste of form. His associates at the Basel School of Design added significantly to my understanding. Paul Rand has, since our first acquaintance, inveighed against my verbal excesses and jargonizing; I appreciate his passion for simple clarity—I hope he finds some of the veil lifted here! Karl Gerstner's work with programmatic design, morphologies, and systems relative to typography and color has visibly influenced those aspects of this book. Wolfgang Weingart has been an important part of my "continuing education."

As is widely known, teachers learn more than students, and it would be wrong not to express my deep gratitude to the many students over the years who have added to my experience, and specifically to those who have contributed examples to this book. Their work is acknowledged where it appears. I am grateful to The University of the Arts for an environment in which to freely work out a program for teaching graphic design, and to George Bunker, with whom a chance meeting led to a long association with what is now the University. I am indebted to my colleagues of the faculty whose brilliant work in both teaching and practice is a constant inspiration and challenge. Hans-U. Allemann has been especially generous with support and advice. Jan Almquist, William Longhauser, Tom Porett and Peter Rose have given valuable feedback on specific chapters.

I would be remiss if I did not pay homage to the software designers whose products have been a source of great amazement and utility in my work on this book and for the Apple Macintosh as my faithful (mostly) right-hand assistant.

A grant from the University of the Arts Venture Fund permitted the pilot run of examples for the chapter on color, printed in the Borowsky Center for Publication Arts at the University.

A grant from the National Endowment for the Arts made it possible for me to devote a sabbatical year to developing the contents.

The impetus for choosing the subtitle "... *universal to Unique,*" first applied to a symposium at The University of the Arts, came from a reading of Jeremy Campbell's *Grammatical Man*, loaned to me by my friend and client, Don Ziegler. From this I realized that Nature is in fact extravagant—wasteful, we might think—as her prodigious output of both species and populations attests, and that for creativity to flourish, for discoveries to occur, a lot of attempts have to be made.

Naturally, I am very grateful to Amanda Miller and Lilly Kauffman of Van Nostrand Reinhold for their enthusiasm for the project, and to the editorial and production staffs—especially Vincent Janoski—for their understanding and patience in bringing the many parts of a complicated book to reasonable consistency without losing the intended ideosyncrasy.

Finally, producing a book that is so completely personal a statement as this easily takes a toll on family life. The support and tolerance for the marathon of writing, designing, and production by my wife, Eleanor, has given me a great lift. And I shouldn't forget her inspiring singing downstairs as I spent many an evening at the computer. She has interrupted many of her own creative activities for editing and proofreading—and reminders to get out of "that deadly passive voice." My daughters Stephanie and Christine contributed their editing talents and good judgment.

To others who have contributed and who may not be properly acknowledged, either here, in the text proper, or in the crediting of sources at the end of the book, my sincere apologies. These errors will be corrected in future editions to the extent they are known.

# **P** r e f a c e

Design history is to creative new beginnings what memory is to experience: glossed, reduced, optimized, idealized.

In a world of appropriation, imitation, revivals, forgeries, of copious information exchange, of quotation of quotation of quotations, of myriad results seen out of context, the key question in learning is: where do we start?

The admonition from some practitioners and some educators in the world of visual design—certainly the example of many practitioners is—steal!

In any culture the Zeitgeist is going to be the determinant for conventions of expression. There is a legitimate place for the communal evolution of the language of form. We draw from and build on the experience of others. And the line between valid influence and flagrant exploitation is not always easy to draw. But the best assurance that authenticity—not quick fixes—will prevail is that people have learned what it means to make something from an apparent nothing, out of their own perceptual and cognitive processes.

This is what this book is about.

Who is it for?

Learners, seekers. It doesn't really make any difference whether they are lay persons, students, or practitioners in the arts. Typically people in the graphic design field. But I get inspired by music, by architecture, by dance, by industrial form, by sculpture and painting. So I hope the evolution of graphic expression finds parallels in other areas of art and design, can resonate with and inform them as well.

The purpose, then, is not to offer exercises to be replicated by others—that would contradict its very essence. Rather the book shows some patterns and principles for structuring problems that I have found useful both in teaching and personal explorations and demonstrates them in concrete terms. They show a way of thinking and working, to the limited extent this is possible in book form. First and foremost, I hope to encourage the plumbing of one's own depths and the building of trust in experienced reality; should this be achieved, my goal will have been reached in the most gratifying terms.

"There can be no mental development without interest . . . .
Joy is the normal healthy spur for the *élan vital* . . . .
The habit of active thought, with freshness, can only be generated by adequate freedom . . . .
The discipline, when it comes, should satisfy a natural craving for the wisdom which adds value to bare experience."
—Alfred North Whitehead

"'School,' for me, is an institution which, through a certain teaching program, attempts to clarify certain information. This information is essentially independent from the concrete demands made by existing professional standards. The teaching programs are open, not bound by fixed opinions. The content of the program is determined and constantly developed in the school. It is important that 'school' maintains an experimental character. The students should not be given irrevocable knowledge or values, but instead, the opportunity to independently search for such values and knowledge, to develop them, and learn to apply them."
—Wolfgang Weingart

The higher the volume, the lower the mortality rates. This way of characterizing the economics of medicine is true of any activity. It takes a while to work out the kinks. Anything seen the first time is ugly, said Picasso. All the more reason that launching a creative career should be protected while the probes into the unknown take place.
—kh

The future of design is beyond pre-conception if it is seen at any given time as the confluence of forces. All I can say with certainty is that I am prevented by my philosophy to repeat history. Certainly this pertains to image characteristics. But this does not exclude retaining those essential values that persist and link us to all humanity and time.
—kh

Our ultimate purpose in design, as usually seen, is to serve society through its commercial and cultural institutions.

Schools are places where we build a sense of the ideal, or better said, where we imagine the potential of the real, practice the processes of intelligent and mind-expanding play and heuristics until formidable obstacles become a challenge that we do not just accept but seek and choose. I call this "real world 2," the world of the exercise of the mind, to distinguish from the world of commerce, too often thought of as *the* real world.

To build an attitude of problem solving that allows seeing the larger context and formulating approaches that have an underlying, systematic structure requires sufficient isolation to allow the deep understanding of the relationship of constants and variables. It needs enough time to get beyond the intimidation of structure to be playfully, imaginatively, self-surprisingly productive in it.

Education addresses fundamental areas of preparation: the understanding and use of the elements of visual form and syntax; the potential for the expression of meaning through visual form; the synthesis of form and meaning in boundaries of time, format, the cooperation and competitiveness of the classroom, the catalytic action of the teacher and, not least, the student's own makeup, intelligence, and prior education.

In a real sense, all human activity takes place in an economically determined or conditioned context. A semester-long course is an economic unit. It is not a good course or a bad course if it lasts a semester and might deal with only one project. It depends rather on what is taught and learned that is of absolutely fundamental and far-reaching character and on what ability is developed to transcend the original confines of the problem, to generate from it that range that is ultimately practical and desirable. Here it is

the quality of the teaching—whether vital or inert—and the confluence of forces in a student's life that will be decisive.

Education that is predictable is not education but training. Of course, education should give a firm grasp of the knowns that form the background of information and the skills that allow the beginning designer to evaluate and research a problem, to proceed systematically toward a solution, and to function in a productive synergistic relationship with others.

But the outcome of true education is unpredictable, either in determining the designer's niche or the effect on professional practice. An intense personal search can surpass in impact (including sales!) those mediocrities that might ensue from merely fulfilling marketing program demands.

**Principles and Practice**

Learning takes place in two basically different ways. In the most common way, we are exposed to something—either a behavior pattern or new information—and we absorb it until its use is natural to us. "Do something often enough, and you will learn how to do it." We immediately sense the value of this kind of learning. It's practical; it fits into existing patterns.

Learning happens in a different way when we impose an intentional distance from the way things are routinely done. If the process is a good one, this approach is not less practical; in fact, it is potentially the most practical because it relates better to any new situation. Innovative solutions result most often from a command of basics and essentials, but these essentials are often blurred by the surface level at which most professional practice tends to function. The ideal is to be capable both with theory—being able to speculate about something and knowing how

**Learning that builds from a solid foundation is state of the art.**
**—kh**

"Japan loves new styles from the West—kitsch, fads, that come and disappear quickly. But behind the scenery, there are hidden principles, a determination to accommodate these changes within the stable image we have inherited."
**—Fumihiko Maki**

"The more fundamental or basic is the idea one has learned, almost by definition, the greater will be its breadth of applicability to new problems."
**—Jerome Bruner**

to set up a framework for testing it—and pragmatics, applying it to common needs.

Certain skills which are supremely valuable from a practical viewpoint can best be learned in an isolated setting if the processes are kept fluid and do not become overly result-oriented. The projects presented in this book are examples of studies in the real world of perceptual comparison where other and equally valid realities of professional practice are not part of the equation. Such real factors in professional practice—client, audience, market, and cost effective-ness—are often too imprecise for consideration in the classroom and can be simulated only at the expense of seriousness and authenticity. In an isolated study environment, personal skills in the formal and technical areas can develop freely.

Educators talk about the need to be generalists. Practitioners want specific and unique results. William Blake said of generalists, "To Generalize is to be an Idiot. To particularize is the Alone Distinction of Merit. General Knowledges are those Knowledges that Idiots possess." Or, as Anatole France puts it: "Truth lies in the nuances." These are sobering words for theoreticians: to me it means that when you learn something you have to act on it—down to the nuances.

Alfred North Whitehead said, "Ideas which are not utilized are positively harmful. By utilizing an idea, I mean relating it to that stream, compounded of sense perceptions, feelings, hopes, desires, and of mental activities adjusting thought to thought, which forms our life."

With these caveats in mind, we could set down the following learning goals that underlie an environment in which we exclude simulated demands and pressures of professional practice:

*1. Principles.* Learning principles from specifics is the basis for information which can transfer from one situation to another. Take for example the principle that clustering functions as contrast against dispersion. If, without being aware of what makes the design succeed, we randomly or spontaneously seize on a design solution that happens to use this underlying principle successfully, we will have appropriated it only as style. And the basis for solving the next problem—the understanding of that principle—has eluded us. Principles are a way of finding order in the kinds of chaotic situations that we often face.

Vital knowledge is transferrable knowledge, not only within the traditional confines of a field but across boundaries that divide fields. Learning principles does not guarantee making connections. What makes the difference is how we deal with these issues—inertly and routinely or in a vital, potential, dynamic way.

*2. Relationship.* An ability to combine diverse visual elements so the parts keep their individual clarity while helping to form a richer whole can only contribute to clarity and sanity. It parallels the ecological attitude that abhors waste and extravagance. Ecologically resolved forms show a timelessness in which all forces in a communication are integrated. This may seem to run counter to the ephemeral quality of most contemporary communication. But regardless of the temporary quality of most communication graphics, their ubiquitous presence presents an opportunity to bring visual quality and aesthetics into our everyday lives.

We might see here a metaphor for a functioning community. Formal elements function as a "society," the components as individuals with unique importance.

"In the architecture of my music I want to demonstrate to the world the architecture of a new and beautiful social common-wealth. The secret of my harmony? I alone know it. Each instrument in counterpoint, and as many contrapuntal parts as there are instruments. It is the enlightened self-discipline of the various parts, each voluntarily imposing on itself the limits of its individual freedom for the well-being of the community. That is my message. Not the autocracy of a single stubborn melody on the one hand, nor the anarchy of unchecked noise on the other. No, a delicate balance between the two; an enlightened freedom. The science of my art. The art of my science. The harmony of the stars in the heavens, the yearning for brother-hood in the heart of man. This is the secret of my music."
—Johann Sebastian Bach

 . . . Is there a sound addressed not wholly to the ear?
We half close
our eyes. We do not
hear it through our eyes.
It is not
a flute note either, it is the relation
of a flute note
to a drum. I am wide
awake. The mind
is listening.
—William Carlos Williams

3. *Structural Base.* Confronting new situations with a structural framework allows us to proceed without a preconceived idea of what the outcome must be. To know in advance how something should be is the biggest deterrent to creative problem solving. Conversely, however, when we do not know the result in advance, a structure prevents the decay of the process into pure chaos.

It is most essential to understand the fundamental realities of contrast and similarity, difference and identity, as a basis for defining relationship. To comprehend the unity of opposites is especially demanding. It is essential, too, to develop a functional understanding of common modes of organization such as hierarchies, progressions, symmetries, grids, and matrices. Being able to apply different base structures is one of the virtues of controlled experiments. At a structural level it is also easier to cultivate a holistic sense of the interplay of arts and sciences. When we understand structure at a most basic level, we become aware of underlying structures in other areas. It opens levels of understanding that previously seemed intimidating or obscure.

4. *Visual Language.* We cultivate the generally shared and underlying language of vision—point, line and plane, module, proportion, sets, rhythm, scale, dimensionality, spatial quality, texture, color, series, direction, motion, confrontation, symbol, metaphor. Properly understood, this knowledge helps us to a true appreciation for the forms of the past and of other cultures because it relates to them in a more essential way than style. It also allows meaningful exchange between teacher and student as well as among students because the language is objective, as opposed to the language of personal like and dislike. It

also helps us to see primary visual qualities regardless of whether the expressive form is representational or abstract.

5. *Range.* It is essential to develop an understanding of the extent of possibilities for transformation and for the range of representation from symbolic to naturalistic. We also need to know and experience the extremes of order and chaos—and points on the continuum between—to recognize when an expression needs greater calming or more excitement. Morphologies are useful for studying a range of alternatives. In this way we set up contexts for feedback, where we can compare qualitative judgments of progressively subtle distinctions objectively.

6. *Sequence.* A sequence of problems gradually increasing in complexity allows the immediate utilization of information gained in a previous step. This gives a sense of purpose and builds personal confidence. In a sequential process, we do not exclude leap-frogging—where it is often possible suddenly to realize connections among what seemed to be exclusive parts. Rather, it is made more possible by the structural seedbed that has been laid, and it is all the more evident when it occurs.

7. *Meaning.* Underlying all of graphic design is finding the message content of visual form and making it optimally experienced. The function of words either as criteria or as content is crucial. This means being sensitized to how visual form correlates with verbal meaning, and learning the power of the visual to create fundamental and swift impressions in ways that words cannot. Contrast provides the most effective context for bringing out meaning. Words of fundamental contrast open the way for a visual statement in which the viewer senses the presence of

"I remember the experience of the adjacencies of opposites.
That was a new concept—
    a new experience which then became a concept
        (perhaps the experience was preceded by the concept)—
            that all things are in the reach of the human mind,
                and that to connect is a mental act,
                    depending on the will to connect.
If I don't want to connect your nose tip with your earrings, I don't.
However, if I wish to connect it, I can do it."
    —Stefan Wolpe

"To produce news of difference, that is, *information*, there must be two entities (real or imagined) . . . . There is a profound and unanswerable question about the nature of those "at least two" things that between them generate the difference which becomes information . . . . Each alone is a non-entity . . . an unknowable, . . . a sound of one hand clapping."
—Gregory Bateson

". . . Bach's development of a musical composition nearly always moved from the simple to the complex, from the general to the specific, from calm to agitated—and almost never in the opposite direction."
—Alfred Dörr, trans. by the author

meaning before anything is deciphered. It seems especially useful to choose words with a near visual equivalence. Using a semantic differential scale such as that used in chapter three or using contrast pairs as in chapters three, four, and five are examples of using content in an identity/difference framework. Chapters six and seven show other ways of using key words as criteria.

8. *Constraints as Openings.* It is crucial to embrace constraints such as limitations of color, typeface, or format as a means to creativity rather than an inhibiting force. It is also necessary to learn to see through limitations and to sense when they are either invalid or purely arbitrary. Laws can either shackle or ensure a life of freedom. Design benefits when we see limitations—to the extent they have been found reasonable— as possibilities rather than as hostile encroachments which need somehow to be violated in order to express creativity. Valid limitations can have positive potential within them. This attitude is pivotal: to choose actively and make something unique out of what is given.

The constraints applied in the projects in this book are only examples of limitations; different constraints yield totally different results. Some are inherent to a project; others are more or less arbitrary decisions in order to give boundaries, even if only temporarily, until a feel for the subject is established.

Once constraints are understood as positive parameters, we are better prepared to make our own games with appropriate rules and structure or to deduce these from our intuitive actions.

9. *Material Quality and Craft.* Developing superior manual and technical skills in the handling of media as an integral and organic part of the conceptual process is the assumption of truly creative work. We try to develop an awareness of the need for precision as part of a progressive concern for clarity rather than an imposed (professional) demand. This removes perfectionism as an end in itself. It means that thinking and doing will harmonize to find the appropriate expression, that perfected craft is not placed ahead of the maturing of the concept; nor conversely, that craft lags behind concept. This may seem to be an obsolete ideal, with computers on one hand and division of labor on the other removing the need for a high personal level of craft. But even in the situations where others may execute aspects of design, the experience of having personally been responsible for completing the cycle of development gives designers greater authority in their liaisons to other persons in a team or with manufacturers and producers.

10. *Concealing/Revealing.* Good projects sensitize us to the rhythmic undercurrent in all material and processes, and to the place and importance of paradox. The paradoxical rhythm of concealing/revealing belongs to communication because generating interest is one of its key functions. It means as much to withhold information as to give it. Processing an image requires that it is in some way foreign, incomplete, unexpected. This processing as a result of questioning is the way a form becomes etched in the mind. The Eiffel Tower, now beloved, was once decried when its unfamiliar design caused consternation and bafflement but ultimately has made an indelible, deep impression. This is equally true of most successful logotypes (and why many of the truly great ones are never realized); corporate decision makers do not have the patience for the etching power of processing and internalizing an image even though ultimately it pays off.

**"When food was scarce, brooding thoughts were distracted by comic tales and string games, for nothing good comes from self-pity. 'Those who know how to play can leap over the hardships of life with ease,' says an Eskimo proverb."**
**—label from an Inuit (Eskimo) exhibition of string games**

**"If you look back at the architecture and design of the last couple of generations, architects who have been invited to work without limits, or given only moderate ones, have almost never yielded first-rate buildings. Indeed, the opposite is closer to the truth: Almost every time an architect has designed a house on a virtually unlimited budget, the result has been one of his or her weakest designs."**
**—Paul Goldberger**

## Form

The characteristics that distinguish one visual mark from another, including shape, size, color, and texture.

## Fixed Forms

Ready-made elements whose finished or primary form is predetermined. In graphic design, typographic fonts are examples of predetermined ready-mades. Ready-mades can range from more universal forms to heavily stylized alphabets and clip-art. The more that stylistic quality is a characteristic of the ready-made, the less room for personal creativity. There is a major difference between type styles which try not to interfere with the word message and those where the lettering style is primary and distracting.

## Content

The underlying thought that provides the criterion and stimulus for a form. Content is the permission for the form of the message. As content changes through cultural evolution, formal renewal is the natural consequence. Because it requires an open, listening mind to engage any new content and present it in a new form, the tendency is to appropriate old content (and old forms) to avoid the challenge.

## Context

The environment—cultural or physical—in which a message or form is perceived and by which it is conditioned. Recognizing, and responding to, changing content and context is the best deterrent to merely decorative, nostalgic, stylistic, or aesthetic design.

## Concept

The structuring of a relationship among forms and messages to achieve a specific expression within a given context.

## Structure

The basis of formal relationships. When defined structurally, a form can be described and analyzed. The fundamental terms of a structure are difference and identity. Identity (similarity) is the unifying principle; difference (contrast) is the means for conveying meaning.

## Matrix

A kind of structure which places information on coordinates, usually—though not necessarily—horizontal and vertical. Connections among elements of information can be read across the whole field in any direction. A matrix is semi- or non-hierarchical. It is a pattern of connections.

## Morphology

A systematic catalog of structural possibilities. By placing a form and its relationship to other forms in a matrix of possibilities, a morphology offers an overview for the kinds of transformations that can be applied to a form. Morphologies, as presented here, are not intended to be absolute matrices of possibilities. Rather, they are flexible devices, which can be customized for the situation.

## Expression

The goal of communication. It should not be confused with mere "effect." An effect may have an entertainment value which will detract from the expression if dominant.

## Personal Commitment and Expression

Involvement grows by keeping an empirical quality in all studies (this is the real world of the studio!). If the investigation is well stated, one can isolate and define a problem for oneself. The resulting clarity enables future action. A structural knowledge speeds up the process of visualizing options because it places the possibilities in context and enlarges the range.

The relationship between the general and specific, implied in the previous discussion of learning goals, is expressed in the contrast of universal and unique. We can find the same contrast in other conceptual pairs:

| general: | specific: |
|---|---|
| universal | unique |
| altruistic | competitive |
| sharing | owning |
| compassionate | egocentric |
| human-centered | consumption-centered |
| ideal | real |
| diffuse | focussed |

Naturally, we seek a balance between these poles.

Personal expression can be an unwanted, egotistic, superimposed quality in design. There is another way. By responding with sensitivity throughout a process, the designer's mark is progressively and naturally given to the work without forcing a personal style on it. While the final product is born more from its inherent content than from the designer's caprice, in a truly organic process it will also reveal unmistakably the personality and sensitivity of the designer.

## The Power of Basics

The basic geometric elements of visual design—triangle, square, and circle—are keys to many more complex forms. Great architects—Le Corbusier, Louis Kahn, I. M. Pei—often revert to basic forms, and thereby renew the vision for architectural form. In fact, Le Corbusier and Frank Lloyd Wright both attended Froebel kindergartens where basic geometric solids were looked upon as "gifts" that were a key to development of the person. Basic elements are rich sources whose final denouement is conditioned by specific content, sites, and materials.

The vocabulary of basics is larger than these three forms, of course. They are formulated differently by different practitioners. Kandinsky, another artist with Froebel kindergarten experience, defined visual basics as point, line, and plane. It is interesting that the basic menus of computer paint programs acknowledge these basic forms. But as computer programs get more elaborate and all kinds of manipulation become easily available, confusion among basic form, transformations, and stylistic mannerisms grows. Consequently work on the computer tends to be excessively colored by what the programs allow one to do versus what is actually appropriate to content and integrated into the whole image.

For the purpose of this book, *basic* is the state of any form in its naked, most anonymous and unglamorous condition. It is analogous to a seed pending germination and nurturing when it is modest and perhaps pathetic in appearance but conceals disproportionate energy and growth. In its relative anonymity, it is more universal; in its flowering and fruition, it culminates its uniqueness. The unique is valid only when it in turn resonates with the universal, where the individual artist/designer identifies with larger humanity.

**The universal/Unique
Process Pyramid:**

**the flowering and fruition of form
in a cyclical rhythm of expansion and
contraction**

| | | |
|---|---|---|
| 1 | seed ..................... | universal (basic form) |
| 2 | seedbed ................ | information |
| 3 | germination .......... | concept |
| 4 | branches .............. | play with alternatives |
| 5 | flowers ................. | moments of focus |
| 6 | pollination ........... | expansion, crossover |
| 7 | fruit ..................... | culmination of form |
| 8 | seed ..................... | reversion to universality |

4

3

2

1

> *"The ultimate object of design
> is form."*
> **—Christopher Alexander**

## Form and Formalism

It is *form* that nudges, stimulates, stirs the mind.

*Form has content.* Form says something inherently—among other things, essential basic qualities of direction or density or texture or size or shape or color.

*The mind seeks meaning in form.* The inquisitive mind tries to find a meaning in whatever it sees. Finding meaning is an act of sanity and self-preservation for human beings in general, as Victor Frankl showed in his book, *Man's Search for Meaning.* He calls this ability *will-to-meaning*, which, if frustrated, leads to neurotic disorders.

*Form kindles meaning.* Viewers who question what they see are the best audience, because they are processing the message. If the psychological or temporal distance between giving and receiving a message is too great, or if the connection to the intended meaning is too absurd, it could all fall apart. Form can arouse, excite, propel, impel meaning. The meaning of form can contradict content, and in a culture where labeling is used so insistently to vouchsafe a meaning, it very often does. Bringing form and content into harmony is a primary concern in all communication.

*Formalism tends toward the decorative.* By formalism, we mean a strict adherence to predetermined forms. The more decorative the form, the less communicative it is and the more it is experienced as merely pleasing, or as an image from which information is optional. Decorative form is characterized by style dominating content.

## Process

Because our senses are incessantly bombarded with outside stimuli delivered in specific stylistic form, it is almost impossible to preconceive a visual form without heavy influence from these stimuli. Because preconceived ideas rely heavily on that which already exists, a clearing of the mind precedes investigations into essentials. A process for the evolution of appropriate form from essential beginnings needs to be learned.

It should be a process that allows for step-wise maturing of a statement but does not exclude spontaneous occurrences or accidental discoveries. It is easy to get stuck on preconceived ideas that seemed brilliant at first but then often block subsequent movement and therefore creativity. The danger in premature resolution is that the problem in its total extent has not been realized.

Chance and quasi-chance operations are another way for a form to originate from within the process rather than as a superimposed style—an aspect of form gets determined by an event only partially controlled by the maker.

The computer is a source for unpredictable shifts and transformations which happen through image truncation at different magnifications; blanking of image by boxes, overlaps, and superimpositions; selection of effects such as partial image reversal; the animated building of an image during screen refreshes; and many others. In using simple cut-and-paste operations, the effect of discarding and cumulatively layering discards can also yield an accumulation of related forms whose relationship has been determined more by chance than choice. While these happenings rarely can be used exactly as encountered, they are nevertheless a strong and important stimulus to the process. They provoke fresh insight into what is possible.

A good process keeps the mind alert. We progressively layer the material, prepare the way for connections to occur, and get ready for intuitive actions that are informed and appropriate—preventing us from jumping to conclusions prematurely. And while process is more important than result, we expect a good result from a good process.

**"In the classic historic tension between the Gnostics (who believed in personal experience of spiritual realities) and Bishops of the early Christian church (who believed in dogmatic authority), drawing lots was the Gnostics' way of circumventing the absolute authority of bishops and priests."**
**—Elaine Pagels**

**A chance operation is a way to open a process, a group, a mind to an undogmatic, larger reality. In a lattice or matrix, positions, responsibilities, gifts are constantly in flux.**
**—kh**

5

6

7

8

## Structure and Freedom

The artist's self-conscious recognition of his individuality has deep effect on the process of form-making. Each form is now seen as the work of a single man, and its success is his achievement only. Self-consciousness brings with it the desire to break loose, the taste for individual expression, the escape from tradition and taboo, the will to self-determination. But the wildness of the desire is tempered by our limited invention. To achieve in a few hours at the drawing board what once took centuries of adaptation and development, to invent a form suddenly which clearly fits its context—the extent of the invention necessary is beyond the average designer.

A person who sets out to achieve this adaptation in a single leap is not unlike the child who shakes his glass-topped puzzle fretfully, expecting at one shake to arrange the bits inside correctly. The designer's attempt is hardly as random as the child's, but the difficulties are the same. His chances of success are small because the number of factors which must fall simultaneously into place are enormous. —Christopher Alexander

The early answer for the architect Christopher Alexander was hierarchical thinking, a tree structure that sorted out primary, secondary, and other factors. Later he wrote "A City Is Not a Tree," an essay which placed elements into a semilattice or interactive matrix to reflect a more dynamic interaction characteristic of real life.

While a tree structure showing successive branchings is dramatically clear and thus very useful, it is obviously also an authoritarian concept. A pure lattice, on the other hand, tends to be anarchic, with every node pulled equally in every direction. An effective structure recognizes hierarchies, but recognizes also how actions may bridge across categories for the good of the total organization. This is the essential feature of the semilattice.

In his book *Structuralism*, the psychologist Jean Piaget defines structure and its properties as "a system of transformations. Inasmuch as it is a system and not a mere collection of elements and their properties, these transformations involve laws: the structure is preserved or enriched by the interplay of its transformation laws, which never yield results external to the system nor employ elements that are external to it. In short, the notion of structure is comprised of three key ideas: the idea of wholeness, the idea of transformation, and the idea of self-regulation.

"The discovery of structure may, either immediately or at a much later stage, give rise to formalization. Such formalization is, however, always the creature of the theoretician, whereas structure itself exists apart from him."

In other words, structures exist. They are the undergirding of all communications whether or not they are named or developed into theories. What appears on the surface to be antistructure in the vernacular expressions shown on the next pages is really the manifestation of the structure in a way determined by materials, skill, and accident, or the unconscious at work.

Structure is an antidote for entropy or breakdown, because while a first impulse may carry insight and inspiration, the reworking will often deteriorate unless the structure is self-consciously understood. In self-conscious design, structure is a "parent." Le Corbusier thought of the plan as the "mother of the building."

Structural understanding is closer to literacy than is stylistic name-dropping. Claude Lévi-Strauss contended that the structuring ability of humans was their distinguishing characteristic (which makes "primitive" people with oral traditions literate—and in many instances wiser!).

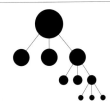

A tree structure shows levels of authority clearly, but it does not allow for a lower-level function to rise above its level or vice versa.

**The structure of authority**

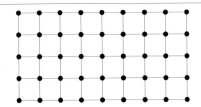

A pure lattice or matrix is not useful for describing dynamic interactions in which different functions and their relationships are described.

**The structure of the anarchist or decorator**

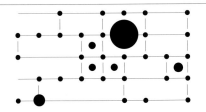

A semilattice is a structure that reflects a dynamic organization. Nodes can be shifted in position and prominence, and units can simultaneously belong to more than one subset. Different readings of the same information are possible.

(To make an analogy, the synapses of the brain are multibit—not just on-off. They are interactive with other synapses to different degrees. Therefore, there are shifting fields of interconnection. Memory is not in a specific location in the brain, but it seems rather to be an interaction that can use synapses in various combinations.)

**The structure of the seeker— of communication**

> *". . . we should never be interested in 'problems of form' as such, as if a form ever arose out of formal problems alone or . . . as if a form ever came into existence [merely] for the sake of the stimulus it would produce."*
> —Walter Benjamin

Structures make sense; they are in some way logical. If rock music is "raging illiteracy," as I have heard it described, how much of what is called "design" in our society is that? This implies a missing sense of logical or grammatical correctness.

Yet we also know and feel that true structures and true expressions are not *only* logical. They have another dimension, verified by the subconscious. Wendell Berry states that "to be divided against Nature, against wildness . . . is a human disaster because it is to be divided against ourselves. It confines our identity as creatures entirely within the bounds of our own understanding, which is invariably a mistake because it is invariably reductive. It reduces our largeness, our mystery, to a petty and sickly comprehensibility." Casaubon in *Foucault's Pendulum* suggests that the sublime exists beyond the encompassable: "if you move in the refined time of revelation, do not follow the fussy, philistine chains of logic and their monotonous sequentiality."

A knowledge of structure leads to connectedness of knowledge, and connectedness leads to intuition, because the pathways are open. Assimilation, we have to remember, is qualitatively different from—and very much slower than—appropriation. Structure is the means to assimilation. A student who had no prior affinity for chemistry reported that one day it dawned on her that it was all really just a matter of proportion, after which the barrier to learning was broken. Proportion is another way to speak of structure. Neither structures, nor the messages they carry, are arbitrary. New Wave graphics brought us a dangerously arbitrary language; to the extent this is true, it is only a wave. (Yet there may be a rightness in this language speaking for our time, in spite of—or because of—its seeming disdain for content.)

## Simplicity and Complexity

Simplicity and complexity are both desirable traits. But simplicity without depth is empty, and complexity without coherence is wasted. A simple image can be richly complex if the parts relate in different ways so that they belong simultaneously to different sets. In the photograph below, the chimney and the arrow are recursive forms, each having a shaft and a point. This set of two related forms is the dominant one of the photograph. But the arrow, as a long horizontal unit, is also related to other long horizontal units forming another set; likewise the bands of gray, including the sky, and the dark textured bands at the lower and mid right. The striation of the chimney shaft picks up the striation of the horizontal banding; the coarse, dark texture at lower right relates to the fine dark texture at mid-right. The dark stone at the top of the chimney and the whole arrow form a set of delineated dark forms in contrast to the set of fuzzy, textured dark forms at the right.

Movement in a process is a flux between reduction and expansion: reduction, from complex to simple; expansion, from simple to complex. The fact that the photograph can be read in a variety of ways makes a relatively simple image surprisingly complex and interesting. Simplification can be a penetrator, making concise. Or simplification can be a blinder, glossing over and avoiding complex reality.

In education, the student's temptation, and frequently the teacher's, is to confuse simple with dull, and conversely, complex with exciting. The real task is to build a sense of continuum from simple to complex so that in the movement toward complexity, if this should be approriate, there is a preservation of the traces of the original message vital for its viability. But it is also to experience that having a good basis means there is never a reason to be stuck on one solution or approach.

"Signs and symbols are used to isolate concepts from a network. Their design can permit their reabsorption into the network."
—Gary Zukaw

"... the important feature of complexity is that it is made possible by redundancy and generated by rules. The power of a small number of fixed rules to produce an unpredictable amount of complexity is very striking."
—Jeremy Campbell

Are these vernacular statements
structured?
The marred letters, the undulation of a crawl,
geometric apertures, steps, cubes if in their pure
form, are clearly structures.

Are they concepts?
They express their content—they must also be
concepts.

There is something operative here which is
immediate, yet clearly structural.
The structural base is what allows improvisation.
Improvisation without a base structure would be
chaos. The structure permits a semichaos of
surface form.

The persisting question: Does disorderliness and
crudeness on the surface enhance legibility by
avoiding the perfection that alienates?

"The anthropologist
goes forward,
seeking to attain,
through the
conscious, of
which he is always
aware, more and
more of the uncon-
scious."
—Claude Lévi-Strauss

> *"Structure is a 'diagram of forces' for the irregularities of an irregular world."*
> —Wentworth d'Arcy Thompson

## Structure and Vernacular Expression

The universals that govern visual form account for great similarity of basic forms and modes of formal organization across distant cultures. They seem to be programmed into the human mind. They show that there is a basic structure dependence that ensures that an expression is coherent and not arbitrary in the way signs and symbols are strung together. Vernacular forms often suggest a kind of surprising freedom, but on closer scrutiny they are found to be solidly based.

The example of Cycladean vernacular architecture, far left, presents an intriguing "gestalt," a seemingly arbitrary collage of planes and forms. Yet each form is derived from a relatively simple geometric base. It is the combination of these forms in response to the interior space needs, on the one hand, and then the adaptation to a terrain on the other, that makes the result unpredictable. The tension between the fully understandable universal base and the inventiveness of the unique composite form creates a special place in which the play of light further varies the form over time.

One senses that the running paint of the "trash" sign on the barrel was not originally intended, but that when it happened it was accepted. The running paint amplifies the meaning of the word, but, like the Greek house, is a one-of-a-kind that would be ridiculous if duplicated.

The undulation of the letters in the "worms" sign is a sophisticated device that temporarily disturbs legibility of the word in favor of its expression. Breaking the pure logic of the zigzag by expanding the weight of the *O* creates a node that focuses the message while calling attention to another attribute of a worm, its cross-section. This is vastly more interesting than applying the routine professional device of an emphasized initial letter *W*. The rhythm of the letters is complemented by the counterpoint of the arrow sequence below it, which moves from the representational hook and worm to the abstract arrow symbol. We see that the underlying structure is clear and that the surface realization is appropriately nuanced.

(We can ask whether those signs might have gotten better the second time around if the makers had been asked to revise them. Probably not! Becoming self-conscious, the makers may not have had the knowledge to refine them.)

Using rows of bagged nuts in a Greek island market to divide different kinds is a simple formal device. Type style nuances for the two different prices effectively distinguish the two similar rows to a greater degree than changing only the numbers.

The basic rules underlying these vernacular expressions show that "rules have the effect of opening up new realms of activity. They are not strictly mechanisms of cause and effect . . . but leave a system essentially open and incomplete, so that it will always be capable of novelty" (Jeremy Campbell).

---

"Universal grammar sees to it that there are rule systems which are natural, and rule systems which are unnatural, the latter are inaccessible, off-limits. Legs, like languages, are free to vary in relatively superficial ways. They come in many shapes and sizes, some more pleasing to behold than others. But the ways in which they do not vary are of more significance from the point of view of biology than the ways in which they vary . . . constraints are an essential part of any process in which order is of value."

. . .

"The information stored in a single law or rule is vastly greater than the information needed to specify a single event."

. . .

"[Noam] Chomsky regards language as a highly efficient system for processing information, because, while speech itself may be disorderly and corrupted, there is regularity and order just beneath it."
—Jeremy Campbell

"In mythology, an invisible plane supports the visible plane."
—Joseph Campbell

### The Structure of this Book

On a practical level, the structure of this book is based on a grid, which, in modernist design from typography to urban planning, is blamed for deathly uniformity. A cursory thumbing through the book shows in fact a wide variety of compositions, almost none of which disclose the modular grid as a dominant feature. A grid serves its purpose best if it allows for surface images which serve the content uniquely and appropriately.

The principles in adopting any grid for creative use can be summarized as follows:

- Let the grid account for the elements that are legitimately repetitive.
- Let it free the designer to play a game of arrangement in a spatial context.
- Let it be useful for bringing together disparate elements that do not easily fit together.

Zoning is a way of allocating space for a certain function on a fairly predictable basis. To state the concept of zoning positively rather than negatively, as is usually the case, zoning is reserving places within a plan for things to happen. It is the happening and not the confining structure that is expressive.

Each chapter of this book is zoned differently for the specific content of the chapter. In this introduction, for example, rows 2-6 are zoned for the main text, row 1 for main heads or extracted quotes, and rows 7-9 for supplementary quotes and visual examples. The sample page shows how the units are used to define different column widths of the type blocks.

Using a grid to design for specific content involves an attitude that, to borrow from French filmmaker Louis Malle, can be called "privileging the actors, subduing the technicians." The "actors" are the elements playing on the surface; the "technicians" are the guidelines of the substructure, in this case a grid.

What I'm looking for in the surface image is something as fresh as the vernacular Greek Island architecture, something unforeseen, brought to life by the specific circumstance yet based on an underlying structure and vocabulary of forms. (Meanwhile the islanders are trying to overcome the informality and make dull houses like ours.)

### Viewing Distance

At what distance is a visual image "good"? Often the best viewpoint is not the intended one. Times Square, very close in on the signs, can be interesting. From a greater distance it is dazzling and appealing; at the *intended* level of sign legibility, however, it is a comparative disappointment. At the microcosmic level of texture and color there are wonderful details to be found. At the macrocosmic level, there are incredible patterns in the overall effect. At both of these scales, one is very aware of the structural, textural. At human scale, where we're *supposed* to view things, the structureless *effect* predominates.

There is a rule of thumb for viewing work to get the sense of the whole: it says that an image should be viewed from a distance three times the diagonal dimension of the image to achieve synthesis vision (global reading). Making thumbnail sketches at normal reading distance has the great advantage of synthesis vision as compared to working at full scale at the same distance.

It requires constant reminding to view work from sufficient distance to get the whole picture. This book was composed on a 13-inch diagonal monitor giving a page view size of 4 by 5 ¾ inches. The page diagonal is about 7 inches, requiring an eye distance of at least 21 inches for global vision. The optimal distance of 28 inches for avoidance of

---

**The modular grid**     **Customized for the Introduction**     **Actual page**

magnetic radiation is close to the optimum for getting a global view of the page. If, however, a monitor is used which permits full scale viewing of an 8-by-11 inch page with a diagonal dimension of 13 inches, a viewing distance of about 39 inches is required. For a double-page spread, the distance is obviously much greater. Many work spaces, whether conventional or electronic, do not allow easy shifting to longer viewing distances. Changing the viewpoint, besides benefiting the character of the design, is healthier for the eyes and body.

### Intimacy, Discipline, Uniqueness

There seems to be a pervasive attitude that says we can be stirred into imagination by watching. But real learning is not a spectator sport.

We long for intimacy, for deep knowledge, but it is not achieved vicariously, secondhand. The lack of true intimacy is a special problem of our time; so much is revealed and so little absorbed, understood, or actually experienced. People are pushed into experiences they can't have by people who are forced into experiences they themselves can't or don't have.

Reaching intimacy is a lifelong process—long searches, sudden knowing. Inspiration is an event within a process. It synthesizes what is already there, what is built up. Knowing paves the way for discovery and surprise, for recognition, because a rich context has been prepared within which we can make new connections.

Structure is the means for building the matrix, the seedbed. A good structure develops discipline for gaining intimate knowledge, for a command of visual language and its application. Intimacy yields knowledge, but with it also the sense of how little we know about other things. (This is the basis of true and necessary humility in what we do.)

Clear structures are tolerant of other clear structures. Clear structures are fundamental to preserving identity in complex environments where structures are juxtaposed or overlaid.

To get another view of the relation of structure and freedom, we might do well to listen to someone who was instrumental in creating the consciousness that led to one of the greatest moments of freedom in American life—the freeing of the slaves:

> There is a principle which is pure, placed in the human mind, which in different places and ages hath had different names. It is, however, pure and proceeds from God. It is deep and inward, confined to no forms of religion nor excluded from any where the heart stands in perfect sincerity. In whomsoever this takes root and grows, of what nation soever, they become brethren in the best sense of the expression. Using ourselves to take ways which appear most easy to us, when inconsistent with that purity which is without beginning, we thereby set up a government of our own and deny obedience to God whose service is true liberty. (From an essay "Considerations on Keeping Negroes, Part II" by the itinerant Quaker visionary, John Woolman, published in 1761).

Structure is the underlying, fundamental, and universal framework that gives a unique expression any credibility it may have. Quality comes from questioning, and structure is the tireless questioner and feedback source. Since an open structure and an open structural attitude will not produce a preconceived result, the relation to audience is another problem—because the new can certainly be exasperating. It takes time for people to "enjoy today what exasperated [them] yesterday. The transformation is extremely slow, and the slowness is easily explained: how

**"There is one thing in which I feel superior to most men: I am freer and at the same time more compliant than they dare to be. Nearly all of them fail to recognize their due liberty, and likewise their true servitude."
—Hadrian, as reported by Margaret Yourçenar**

**About knowing: In a radio interview with the singer, Benita Valenti talked about making demands on the voice: ". . . it's the brain; . . . if you don't know how to ask something of it, you can't do it. If you do, you can."
—Interview, "Fresh Air"**

could comprehension evolve as rapidly as the creative faculties? It follows in their wake" (Albert Gleizes & Jean Metzinger, *Cubism*). Isn't this true of anything authentic, anything that is a cultural advance?

### Permissive Structure and Play

Intimacy is the basis for permission and freedom, not vice versa.

Structure and meaning are permissions rather than constraints; from them evolve endlessly new forms. The permissiveness of structures and content stems from subject matter itself, and permission is achieved through progressive intimacy. The permission inherent in content makes for an enduringly sound learning experience.

Looking for freedom outside a constraint substitutes one tyranny for another—the tyranny of style or the tyranny of chaos. A structure of constraints can be tyrannical, too. But seeing a constraint as an opening makes it possible to "jump out of the system" at an appropriate, significant, compelling moment.

The key to freedom of expression is agility with the rules. Like playing any game, it takes practice. In any game, the moves can't be purely arbitrary. Structure releases energy and thought while giving direction.

For this to work, discipline and freedom must be in a continual cyclical flux. Eight Texts Under One Roof, the title of the first project in this book, is a way to describe the function of structure: to hold together diverse content while allowing for clear expression of the differences. Each of the projects has a gamelike quality that invites playful risk-taking.

But structure places the experience in a framework where play and purpose join, beyond mere amusement or entertainment.

### Dangers in a Structural Emphasis

◆

*Mediocrity.* Structures can be deadening. We must be clear that the danger of a structure is that it makes mediocre competence easily attainable. Templates as ready-made grids for publications are examples of tools that assist a basic order on the one hand but tend toward mediocrity on the other.

◆

*Alienation.* In our attempts to construct a language, we stand in danger of alienating, justifying a form on the grounds that it is structurally based without testing for clarity. Purely constructed languages (like esperanto) are esoteric oddities. Language has to be adequately based in the prior experience of the group it addresses.

A reductionist approach is useful only if it leads to greater functional recognition. Do structuralists shift the emphasis too much to the syntax of structure as an end in itself rather than as a support for the meaning? Also, we have to realize that "the merely poetic destroys poetry." (Vladimir Holan).

◆

*Excess.* Another danger—one that I have grappled with in relation to the computer—is that a structure, by enabling excessive permutation, may tend to obscure the problem of focus and concentration on a single most vital expression. In a culture of indeterminacy this may seem right, but we need to check it against the historical view: "The parts of a whole stand to each other in a relation of complementarity. They form not merely an aggregate, but an organization, in which several members are mutually implicated in each other. All are necessary, none is dispensable, for the meaning of each is seen to reside in the relations which bind it to those others. The complementarity of parts is

"Not that Watt felt calm and free and glad, for he did not, and had never done so. But he thought that perhaps he felt calm and free and glad, or if not calm and free and glad, at least calm and free, or free and glad, or glad and calm, or if not calm and free, or free and glad, or glad and calm, at least calm, or free, or glad, without knowing it."
—Samuel Beckett

"Rhythm MUST have meaning. It can't be merely a careless dash off, with no grip and no real hold on the words and sense, a tumty tum, tumpty tum tum tum ta . . . . Every literaryism, every book word, fritters away a scrap of the reader's patience, a scrap of his sense of your sincerity. When one really feels and thinks, one stammers with simple speech; it is only in the flurry, the shallow frothy excitement of writing, or the inebriety of a metre, that one falls into the easy—oh, how easy!—speech of books and poems that one has read."
—Ezra Pound

what [we] understand when [we] speak of the 'inevitable-ness' of a work of art: to take from it any part or to add to it any part is to destroy the distinctive kind of equilibrium which it has . . . . Complementarity . . . is the sovereign principle of art" (John F. A. Taylor).

◆

*Mazes.* Finally, a preoccupation with structures can lead to complexities of imagery "creating planes we can't fly." We can be carried away and intrigued by complexity to the point of inextricability, having fallen in love with the maze through which only we can find our way.

In all demonstrations in this book, I have tried to show that the evolution of form from universal, simple beginning points yields great variety and novelty when we understand the transformational potential and take care to only gradually mix factors—the great temptation of the computer age— especially at the beginning.

What is lacking in our world is a sense of rhythm and structure. It is a chaotic scene into which we inject our work. In all these demonstrations I have removed myself from outwardly pragmatic concerns to concentrate on the way form itself carries meaning. This may seem a too rarefied world, but it is the one where visual sense is fortified and prepared for pragmatic application.

In this spirit these demonstrations are offered. Bon voyage!

"Few things are more characteristic of the modern mind than to take complication for improvement. We have automatic windows on our cars, which is a convenience; but on a hot day, or in an accident, they cannot be opened unless the engine is running. The paradox of inconvenient convenience repeats in all domains."
—Jacques Barzun

"An artist does not skip steps; if he does, it is a waste of time because he has to climb them later."
—Jean Cocteau

"Oddities only work when they're to the point." (Casaubon speaking, rejecting the mix of magic and science in *Foucault's Pendulum.*)
—Umberto Eco

" . . . fundamentals stay the same."
—jazz musician Dizzy Gillespie

*"The secret of flexible behavior is to have interesting experiences in stable conditions as free as possible from serious danger.*

*"One of the most important of these experiences is play. Play, which is the normal activity of children who feel secure, is a symptom of versatility that tends to lead to more versatility.*

*"Play is a symbolic activity . . . its rules may be broken, or new rules invented, without leading to serious consequences. . . . In play it is possible to go to extremes, to be daring, to experiment, so that the boundaries of the permissible and the practical can be tested to the full."*
—Jeremy Campbell

# 1.

*Space is the common denominator of a visual composition, the glue. In this project, strict formal limitations are accepted to emphasize the use of space as a dynamic field which contributes directly to the expression of the content.*

*Space is thus the primary factor for bringing diverse texts under one roof.*

All examples are by students of graphic design at
The University of the Arts as noted.
Christopher Ransom assisted in the project.

**• Technical Notes:**
Software: PageMaker®. Pages were saved as
encapsulated postscript (EPS) files and resized as
necessary to bring them into the pages as
reduced scale examples.

The Question of

# size,

*emphasis,*

*and space*

**Educational Goals:**

*To experience space as a primary factor in visual organization.*

*To practice applying a consistent grid format within a given page format.*

*To use the limited graphic imaging tools of a page-layout software program appropriately to develop a unique character for each page.*

*To develop a visual language that both unifies a set of texts and offers the means to diversify the form of each text in relation to the others in the set.*

*To open the exploration laterally by concentrating on a single text.*

*To develop a useful combination of conventional typographic sketching methods with work on a computer terminal.*

*To introduce a page-layout program to students of design who have minimal previous computer experience.*

*To experience the signature limitations of a book format.*

**Pragmatic Goal:**
*To design a booklet integrating eight short texts and a set of eight variations on one of these.*

**Given:**
*A page-layout document containing preformatted texts, each in a block of constant size and positioned within a static grid.*

**Process:**

**1**
*Design a master page for eight given texts. Provide home locations for the text block, head, credit, and a numeral. Devise a means of marking the boundary of the text block using dots and lines. Use ordinary cut, paste, and drawing tools.*
**2**
*Build the set of eight texts. One text may be replaced with a new text that fits the size parameters and adds variety to the set. Compose the master page and the set of eight on the computer. Use the computer to test alternatives and refine the image.*
**3**
*Choose any one of the pages as the basis for a set of eight new variations.*

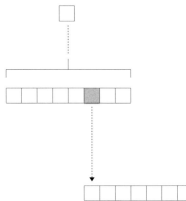

Notes concerning studio procedure:

It is important to experience the reality of imagery on paper and to see experiments comparatively. For this project, students spent approximately two-thirds of their class time in a conventional studio where it was possible to display all the alternatives, to take time to analyze and compare them, to make quick changes using ordinary cut-and-paste procedures.
•
The effect is to relieve an often unproductive, frustrating, and unhealthy obsession with the computer.

It is common to use space as a kind of luxury, projecting generosity or classic simplicity—a formula for "class." But if space is used only as a formula or device, it is also readily suspect as being either wasteful, arrogant, or elitist. Yet space is a human need, and the experience of space is typically an exhilarating one.

Space used as an integral part of design goes beyond formula because it must be conceived as an essential complement to the idea of the text or image—where space is as effective as the type or picture elements in creating the total image. Space then is not background; it is a participant defining proximities and repelling or attracting actions.

We can look at two-dimensional space as a stage within which characters move. They need space for their separate identities, and the control of space describes the tension and harmony among these characters. Seeing the elements as characters creates a societal analogy making the abstraction easier to understand.

Great design creates space. That is to say, elements can be used in such a way that space is occupied, consumed—or they can be used in a way that generates new space in a given environment. The sequence often follows a certain pattern. A first element is placed dynamically into space. Then come the details still to be added. Gradually the original dynamic is spoiled by other elements which literally use up the space. Often the problem comes because there are too many elements, but even after a good editing process has eliminated redundancy and superfluity, the adding of successive elements tends to destroy space.

Integration is the answer, but it isn't easy to attain because the process gets increasingly self-conscious with each new move. If integration is effective, the reader can't miss anything. If the key to a concept of the surface is position in space, every element has its own prominence, regardless of size. It is possible to recast minor elements as major ones, to make every element appropriately prominent, regardless of the size. Size dominance and hierarchy are then inadequate to define ultimate importance.

In this project, headline, text, and source vary minimally in size. None is *less* important than the other. The question for the designer is to present them so that the eye receives all elements with ease, so that each element sparks the presence of the others. At the same time the function— whether as title, body, credit, or folio (page number)—is unmistakable.

The thumbnail size of the examples in this chapter may seem at first absurdly small. The advantage in this scale is that we can read all the elements as abstractions and more readily see space as the glue.

### Dots and Lines

Space is defined by visual elements placed in the space. It helps to be aware of how the space is designed if these elements are defined in abstract terms. The most elementary language for two-dimensional image construction defines forms as dots and lines. These forms can appear in their most basic, extreme, and literal form, as they tend to in this project. But most imagery is inherently more complex than the language of pure dots and lines permits. The Russian painter and theoretician Wassily Kandinsky in his quest to find a systematic base for visual arts that would correspond to that for music, attempted to show that complex forms were variations on these elements. Their separate character and interrelation, he thought, was the underlying basis for graphic painting and design.

I remember vividly attempting to place a cluster of type in a poster while studying with the Swiss educator and designer, Armin Hofmann. We always hand-sketched lettering and typographic representations, trying to get the right weight, size, and action to charge the space. I had just concluded that the total effect of a cluster we were working on was too weak. Hofmann reminded me then that "it wasn't a dot, wasn't a line—(therefore) wasn't anything." The comment was enlightening because the cluster I was creating was actually a dot which was highly differentiated into fine lines. Correcting the weight of dot meant seeing it in its abstract essence. Then the task of bringing up the weight of the inner parts became clear. Hofmann's approach to training the eye to see form abstractly began by dealing with dots and lines in their purest form and progressively modifying and differentiating the forms as new content came into them. This progression is shown in outstanding examples in Hofmann's *Graphic Design Manual*.

The examples in this book are developed out of experience with these basic forms at increasing levels of complexity.

In project 1 the elements are used in a more purely geometric way. The emphasis is on seeing type as lines. In clusters, these lines create together a shape which can be seen as dots if contained enough to have a focal quality, or as planes if large enough to convey mass.

### The Shape of Text

The shape and gray value of type is brought to expression by
  reconciling two forces:

●

The first is the character of the text—its length, its organization and logic, its expressive intention. In many ways, text
  brings with it an inherent shape or shape potential. Before
  any form is given to the text, it is important to know what
  form the text already has. In project 1, for example, the
  recipe (text 2, page 30) has an obvious inherent shape. The
  Piaget text (text 1, page 30), by listing the "three key
  ideas," presents a natural, inherent shape. The Mallarmé
  text (text 6, page 31) follows the author's intention for line
  structure. And so also the other texts used for this project
  have a unique shape quality.

●

The second is the aesthetic-perceptual judgment that
  determines the following:
a. The relationship among the different categories of spaces,
  from letter to word to line to paragraph spacing; the line
  length; the degree of raggedness; and the paragraph signal.
b. The character of the type, its weight, size, style, and slant.
  Too great an emphasis on the style of the type can easily
  obscure the other aspects which have a more fundamental
  effect on the function of a larger composition.
Legibility is the net result of the interaction among all facets.
  In pragmatic problem-solving situations, the aspect that
  tends to to be most neglected is space.

### A Normative Base for Type

One effect of the advent of the computer is that—with the
  options for sizing type, for spacing, for rag control, for
  letter distortion, for stretching to fit—a sense of the
  norms, historically established by the type designer and
  the foundry, is easily lost. Getting regrounded in the good,
  simple, normative base is essential:
● *Letter spacing* that is neither crowded nor loose.
● *Word spacing* that keeps a strong sense of line without
  running words together.
● *Line spacing* which is greater than word spacing.
Line length should be based on legibility. Raggedness should
  be controlled within a range which, while activating the
  page, does not distract from reading. Word spacing should
  not be allowed to fluctuate in ragged settings, since
  evenness of spacing is a prime advantage for legibility.
  Justified text must have a wide enough measure—55-60
  characters minimum—to permit a consistent gray value
  and minimum fluctuation from the legibility norms.
Furnished with texts based on optimum legibility, the
  students are conditioned to the normative as a point of
  departure for their activity. It clears away preconceived or
  stylistic effects.

1. Static grid as given.

2. A custom grid is used to zone the format.
Separate zones are set up for each facet: title,
body text, credit (author and source), number.

3. In the surface design phase, elements from
the limited vocabulary of a page-layout program
are added to provide an expressive dynamic.
The lower boundary of the main text zone is
defined in this case as a row of dots.

*The goal is a free and unique surface structure anchored to the grid.*
*The negative space is implicitly structured by the presence of the grid.*

*—kh*

**Variations in surface design**  A comparison of six approaches to spatial organization and geometric elements applied to "Three Key Ideas," text 1, page 30.

**The Choice of Texts**

Range is a perennial question in design. Darkness is made clear by the presence of light; whimsy, by the presence of profundity; the vernacular, by the presence of the classical. The eight texts were chosen with this in mind.

Any exploration of texts should bring students a new experience in reading and interpreting. For this reason, unfamiliar material is important. We *become* interested in that with which we have sincerely wrestled and which we have viewed from many angles. From this experience it is possible to develop wholly new interests, to realize that things we thought were dry and boring have a potential for expression of which we were first unaware.

In this experience the students at first looked only for formal interest in using the abstract elements. When the potential meaning of form in relation to the texts was read back to them, they were awakened to the texts and their meaning. It was then that they began a new phase of deciphering the texts and making conscious connections in the application of abstract form.

This is not a criticism, because somewhat aimless beginnings—looking only for visual interest—often lead to less forced connections to the material.

**❶**
**Three Key Ideas, by Jean Piaget**

As a first approximation, we may say that a structure is a system of transformations. Inasmuch as it is a system and not a mere collection of elements and their properties, these transformations involve laws: the structure is preserved or enriched by the interplay of its transformation laws, which never yield results external to the system nor employ elements that are external to it.

In short, the notion of structure is comprised of three key ideas:
the idea of wholeness,
the idea of transformation,
the idea of self-regulation.

•
*This text opens the series
and establishes criteria for
the project.*

**❷**
**Lentils with Spinach and Lemon, by Paula Wolfert**

Ingredients:
$1/2$ pound lentils
1 cup sliced onions
$1/4$ cup olive oil
3 cloves garlic, peeled and finely chopped
$1/4$ cup chopped fresh coriander
10 ounces frozen spinach leaves, completely thawed and roughly chopped
2 medium potatoes, peeled and sliced
Salt and freshly ground black pepper
$1/4$ cup freshly squeezed lemon juice, or more to taste

Equipment:
Saucepan with cover
Large stainless steel or
enameled casserole

Working time:
15 minutes

Cooking time:
1 hour 20 minutes

Serves:
6

1. Wash and pick over lentils. Place in a saucepan and cover with water. Bring to the boil. Cook, covered, about 20 minutes.

2. Meanwhile, in a large casserole, brown the onions in oil. Stir in the garlic and coriander. Add the spinach and sauté 5 to 6 minutes, stirring frequently. Add the potatoes, lentils, and enough lentil cooking liquid to cover. Season with salt and pepper. Bring to the boil, lower the heat, and simmer 1 hour or until thick and soupy. Stir in the lemon juice. Serve hot, lukewarm, or cold.

•
*A text characterized by its
concrete quality,
methodical sequence, and
irregular shape.*

**❸**
**IT Tango, by Laurie Anderson**

She said:     It looks. Don't you think it looks a lot like rain?

He said:      Isn't it. Isn't it just. Isn't it just like a woman?

She said:     It's hard. It's just hard. It's just kind of hard to say.

He said:      Isn't it. Isn't it just. Isn't it just like a woman?

She said:     It goes. That's the way it goes. It goes that way.

He said:      Isn't it. Isn't it just like a woman?

She said:     It takes. It takes one. It takes one to. It takes one to know one.

He said:      Isn't it just like a woman?

She said:     She said it. She said it to no. She said it to no one.

               Isn't it. Isn't it just. Isn't it just like a woman?

Your eyes:  It's a day's work to look into them.
Your eyes:  It's a day's work just looking into them.

•
*An amusing and whimsical
text with an undercurrent
of profound male-female
left-right brain dichotomy,
presented in a ritualistic
manner, as it appears on
the record sleeve.*

**❹**
**Cities and Eyes, by Italo Calvino**

When you have forded the river, when you have crossed the mountain pass, you suddenly find before you the city of Moriana, its alabaster gates transparent in the sunlight, its coral columns supporting pediments encrusted with serpentine, its villas all of glass like aquariums where the shadows of dancing girls with silvery scales swim beneath the medusa-shaped chandeliers. If this is not your first journey, you already know that cities like this have an obverse: you have only to walk in a semicircle and you will come into view of Moriana's hidden face, an expanse of rusting sheet metal, sackcloth, planks bristling with spikes, pipes black with soot, piles of tins, blind walls with fading signs, frames of staved-in straw chairs, ropes good only for hanging oneself from a rotten beam.

From one part to the other, the city seems to continue, in perspective, multiplying its repertory of images: but instead it has no thickness, it consists only of a face and an obverse, like a sheet of paper, with a figure on either side, which can neither be separated nor look at each other.

•
*A prose text presenting the
city as having an exotic
but thin face with an
"obverse" of decay. The
text is justified left and
right, showing the notion
of a pristine, flat face.*

**❺**
**Spoken and Written, by Ferdinand de Saussure**

Language and writing are two different systems of signs;
the only purpose of the latter is to represent the former.
Linguistics is not concerned
with the connection between the written and spoken word—
its sole object is the latter: the spoken word.
~~But the written word is so closely bound up with the spoken, whose image it is,~~
~~that it is increasingly arrogating the main role to itself.~~
~~Ultimately the point is reached~~
~~where more importance is attached to representation of the spoken sign~~
~~than to this sign itself.~~
It's like thinking that to know someone,
~~it is better to look at his photograph than his face.~~

•

*De Saussure so valued*
*speaking over writing that*
*he destroyed his lecture*
*notes. The parts of the text*
*referring to the written are*
*therefore struck through in*
*the version furnished.*

**❻**
**From "A Tomb for Anatole," by Stéphane Mallarmé**

o earth — you do not
grow anything
— pointless
— I who
    honor you —

bouquets
   vain beauty

child sprung from
the two of us — showing
us our ideal, the way
— ours! father
and mother who
    sadly existing
survive him as
the two extremes —
badly coupled in him
and sundered
— from whence his death — o-
bliterating this little child "self"

•

*The fragmentation of the*
*text is as created by the*
*poet and relates to the*
*tragic content*
*characterized by the word*
*obliteration.*

**❼**
**Field Forces, by Walter Thirring and Joseph Needham**

Modern theoretical physics . . . has put our thinking about the essence
of matter in a different context. It has taken our gaze from the visible—
the particles—to the underlying entity, the field. The presence of matter
is merely a disturbance of the perfect state of the field at that place;
something accidental, one could almost say, merely a blemish. Accord-
ingly, there are no simple laws describing the forces between elementary particles . . . . Order and symmetry must be sought in the underlying
field.

The Chinese physical universe in ancient and medieval times was a
perfectly continuous whole. *Ch'i* condensed in palpable matter was not
particulate in any important sense, but individual objects acted and
reacted with all other objects in the world . . . in a wavelike or vibratory
manner dependent, in the last resort, on the rhythmic alternation at all
levels of the two fundamental forces, the *yin* and the *yang*. Individual
objects thus had their intrinsic rhythms. And these were integrated
. . . into the general pattern of the harmony of the world.

•

*Context, or field, as a basis*
*for both scientifically and*
*intuitively evolved world*
*views is the subject of*
*these two paragraphs.*

**❽**
**Symmetry, by Matila Ghyka**

. . . "symmetry" as defined by Greek and Roman architects as well
as Gothic master builders, and by the architects and painters of the
Renaissance, from Leonardo to Palladio, is quite different from our
            modern term symmetry (bi-lateral symmetry).
We cannot do better than to give the definition of Vitruvius:
"Symmetry resides in the correlation by measurement between the
various elements of the plan, and between each of these elements
and the whole. . . . As in the human body . . . it proceeds from proportion—the proportion the Greeks called *analogia*—and achieves
consonance between every part and the whole . . . . When every
important part of the building is thus conveniently set in proportion
by the right correlation between height and width, between width
and depth, and when all these parts also have their place in the total
symmetry of the building, we obtain eurhythmy."

Rhythm is in time what symmetry is in space.

•

*Symmetry by this*
*definition has to do with*
*the simultaneity of*
*rhythmic forces rather*
*than the obvious and static*
*bilateral idea.*

The texts were set uniformly to the following specifications:

— **9 pt Helvetica**
— **3 pts leading**
— **90% normal word spacing**
— **normal +3% letter spacing**
— **24 pica line length maximum**
— **page size: 8.25" square**
— **text block unit: 24x39 picas (golden section rectangle)**
— **average line length justified or ragged: 60 characters (except where line-for-line)**

**Basic Set:**
All solutions shown on the following pages maintain the sequence shown here.          —>

Note the distinctive shape of each text and the resulting distinctive spatial form.

The pages are shown in 2-page spreads.

A page marked **X** has been replaced with new content chosen by the student.

**Expansion Set:**
Any one of the first eight pages is chosen as the basis of a further eight-page explora-tion. This expansion set is displayed in the lower half page and indicated by an **X** in the basic set.

If a replacement text was chosen for one of the texts in the basic set, it may also be the basis for the expansion set—or a completely new text may be chosen as on pages 37 and 43. (Replacements in the basic set are indicated by an **R**.)

grid

1 *Three Key Ideas*

2 *Lentils*

3 *IT Tango*

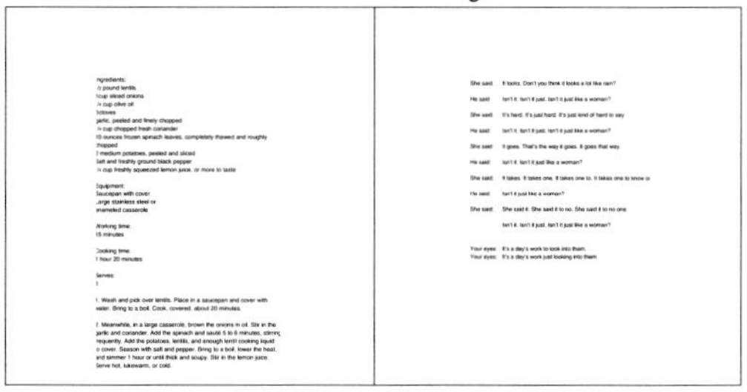

4 *Cities and Eyes*

5 *Spoken and Written*

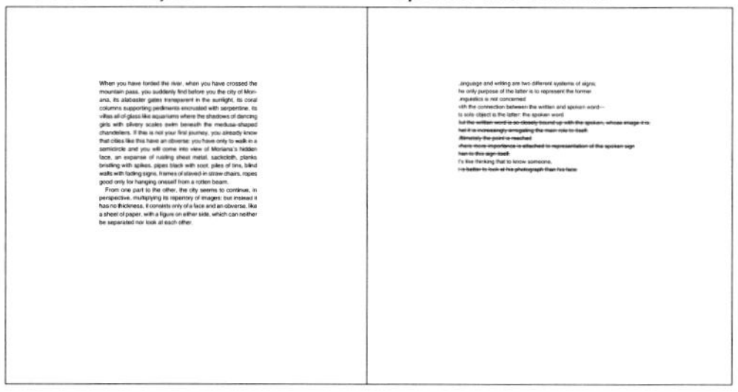

6 *Anatole*

7 *Field Forces*

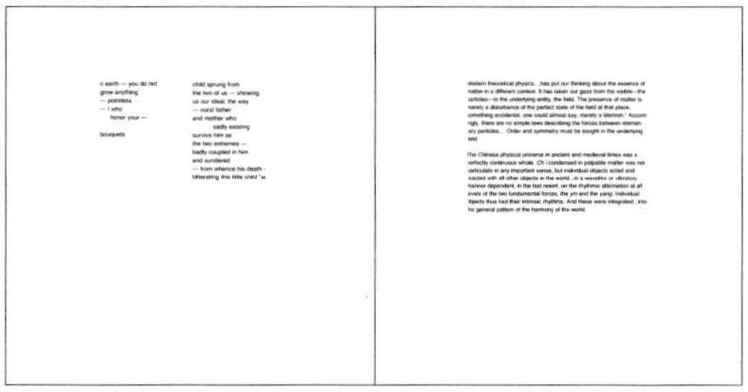

8 *Symmetry*

9

*open*

10

*open*

11

*open*

12

*open*

13

*open*

14

*open*

15

*open*

16

*open*

*The displays on pages 35–47 show the
two sets of eight pages as solved by
seven designers. Selected pages, such as
those below, are enlarged to show detail.*

Field Forces

Modern theoretical physics....has put our thinking about the essence of
matter in a different context. It has taken our gaze from the visible—the
particles—to the underlying entity, the field. The presence of matter is
merely a disturbance of the perfect state of the field at that place;
something accidental, one could almost say, merely a blemish." Accord-
ingly, there are no simple laws describing the forces between elementary particles.... Order and symmetry must be sought in the underlying
field.

④ Statements by Walter Thirring and Joseph Needham,
quoted in Fritjof Kapra, *The Tao of Physics*, Bantam, 1975

The Chinese physical universe in ancient and medieval times was a
perfectly continuous whole. *Ch'i* condensed in palpable matter was not
particulate in any important sense, but individual objects acted and
reacted with all other objects in the world...in a wavelike or vibratory
manner dependent, in the last resort, on the rhythmic alternation at all
levels of the two fundamental forces, the *yin* and the *yang*. Individual
objects thus had their intrinsic rhythms. And these were integrated...into
the general pattern of the harmony of the world.

7 enlargement

14 enlargement

survive him as the

two

ex

t  r  e  m  es

badly coupled in him
and sundered

from whence his death
o- bliterating this little
child

**Features:**

Small dots are displaced from a constant row which defines the text block limit. The displaced dots are used in combination with a single large dot to allude to the content.

For example, for text 1 the idea of wholeness is expressed by the large dot in a key relation to the text.

The idea of transformation is expressed by a dot absorbing the numeral, changing its character.

The idea of self-regulation, of rules, is expressed by the row of dots at the bottom limit of the main text zone. In the first panel the row is complete, then dots are dropped out in response to the varying contents.

grid

1

2

3

4

5

6 **X**

7

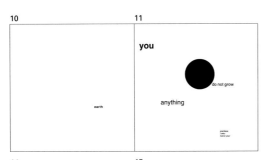

8

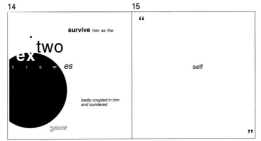

**Expansion on Text 6:**

Variable type size, slant, spacing, and reverses are used to build toward entombment using the Mallarmé text.

9

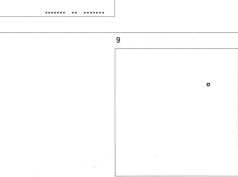

10

11

12

13

14

15

16

Three Key Ideas

As a first approximation, we may say that a structure is a system of transformations. Inasmuch as it is a system and not a mere collection of elements and their properties, these transformations involve laws: the structure is preserved or enriched by the interplay of its transformation laws, which never yield results external to the system nor employ elements that are external to it.

In short, the notion of structure is comprised of three key ideas:
the idea of wholeness,
the idea of transformation,
the idea of self-regulation.

Jean Piaget, *Structuralism*,
Harper and Row, 1970

*1*

1 enlargement

12 enlargement

b                    u                    t

The race is not to the swift, nor the battle to the strong
Good guys finish last.

b                    u                    *t*

God makes a nest for the blind bird
God helps those who help themselves

The meek shall inherit the earth
To those who have is given
Don't cross your bridges until you come to them
Plan ahead

b                    u                    t

Marry in haste, repent in leisure
He who hesitates is lost

Love thy neighbor as thyself
b          Familiarity breeds contempt      u          t

**Features:**
Type reversed out of
corner bleed bar; vertical
bar and credits mark limit
of text block. One dot of
variable size, position, and
cropping moves in relation
to the vertical bar.

grid

1

2

3

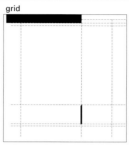

4

5

6

7

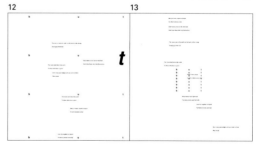

8

**Replacement Text:**
Contradictory proverbs are
placed against varied
(stammering) treatments
of the conjunction "but."

9

10    11

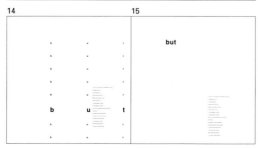

but
but
but
but
but

Don't cross your bridges until you come to them
Plan ahead

The meek shall inherit the earth
To those who have is given

The race is not to the swift, nor the battle to the strong

Good guys finish last

God makes a nest for the blind bird

God helps them who help themselves

Marry in haste, repent in leisure

He who hesitates is lost

12    13

14    15

b    u    t

but

16

but

15 enlargement

meanwhile,

b r o w n the onions

# Stir in:
garlic
coriander

# Add:
spinach
potatoes
lentils

The progressive masking to support the idea of combining was a by-product of seeing text blocks partially obscured on the computer screen, then finding the way to make it effective.

7

**Features:**
Bars of constant length and
variable weight are used in
the left column to create
emphasis as appropriate.
Consistency allows the
exception, text 5, to be
effective. The penetration
into the text space pushes
the written words over,
reinforcing the text.
Reversed type is used in
text 7R, "The Inhabitants,"
which was a replacement
text.

grid

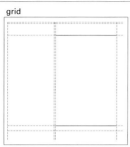

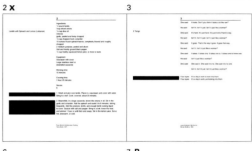

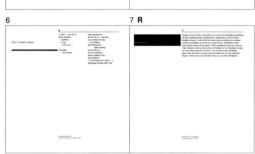

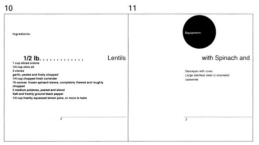

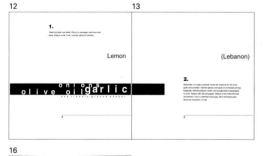

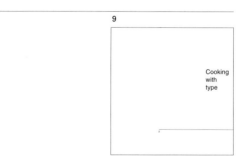

**Expansion on Text 2:**
The recipe is the subject for
a kinesthetic experiment
stretched over 8 pages.

9

Cooking
with
type

10

Ingredients:

1/2 lb. . . . . . . . . . . . .    Lentils
1 cup sliced onions
1/4 cup olive oil
3 cloves
garlic, peeled and finely chopped
1/4 cup chopped fresh coriander
10 ounces frozen spinach leaves, completely thawed and roughly
chopped
2 medium potatoes, peeled and sliced
Salt and freshly ground black pepper
1/4 cup freshly squeezed lemon juice, or more to taste

with Spinach and

Saucepan with cover
Large stainless steel or enameled
casserole

12

1.

Wash and pick over lentils. Place in a saucepan and cover with
water. Bring to a boil. Cook, covered, about 20 minutes.

Lemon

**onions**
**olive oil garlic**

(Lebanon)

2.

Meanwhile, in a large casserole, brown the onions in oil. Stir in the
garlic and coriander. Add the spinach and sauté 3 to 5 minutes, stirring
frequently. Add the potatoes, lentils, and enough lentil cooking liquid
to cover. Season with salt and pepper. Bring to a boil, lower the heat
and simmer 1 hour or until thick and soupy. Stir in the lemon juice.
Serve hot, lukewarm, or cold.

14

| Working time: | 15 minutes |
| Cooking time: | 1 hour  20 minutes |

. . . . . . . . **lentils**
**20 minutes**

15

meanwhile,
b r o w n  the **onions**

**Stir in:**
**garlic**
**coriander**

**Add:**
**spinach**
**potatoes**
**lentils**

16

**Season**
**Season**

s i m m e r    **1 hour**

with  **lemon juice**

Serve hot
Serve lukewarm
Serve cold

**Serves 6**

Spoken and Written

Language and writing are two different systems of signs;
the only purpose of the latter is to represent the former.
Linguistics is not concerned
with the connection between the written and spoken word—
its sole object is the latter: the spoken word.
But the written word is so closely bound up with the spoken, whose image it is,
that it is increasingly arrogating the main role to itself.
Ultimately the point is reached
where more importance is attached to representation of the spoken sign
than to this sign itself.
It's like thinking that to know someone,
it is better to look at his photograph than his face.

5

Ferdinand de Saussure, "Cours de linguistique générale."
Bally and Sechehaye, Lausanne, 1916

"Spoken" is to "written" as undulating is to straight. Undulating (spontaneous) and straight (rigid) rows of dots interweave in this study.

Although the straight row is stronger in weight, the overall effect is dominated by movement, reinforcing the content of the text and De Saussure's position as a linguist.

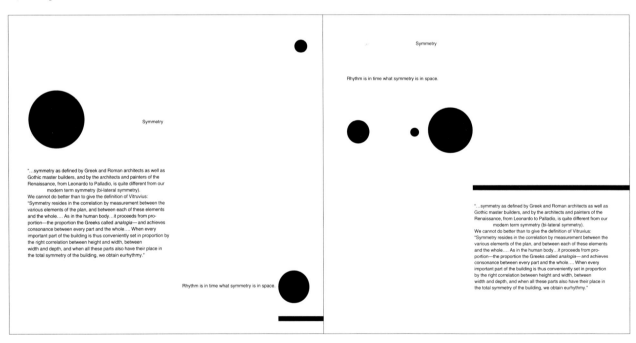

Symmetry

"…symmetry as defined by Greek and Roman architects as well as Gothic master builders, and by the architects and painters of the Renaissance, from Leonardo to Palladio, is quite different from our modern term symmetry (bi-lateral symmetry).
We cannot do better than to give the definition of Vitruvius:
"Symmetry resides in the correlation by measurement between the various elements of the plan, and between each of these elements and the whole…. As in the human body…it proceeds from pro-portion—the proportion the Greeks called *analogia*—and achieves consonance between every part and the whole…. When every important part of the building is thus conveniently set in proportion by the right correlation between height and width, between width and depth, and when all these parts also have their place in the total symmetry of the building, we obtain eurhythmy."

Rhythm is in time what symmetry is in space.

Symmetry

Rhythm is in time what symmetry is in space.

"…symmetry as defined by Greek and Roman architects as well as Gothic master builders, and by the architects and painters of the Renaissance, from Leonardo to Palladio, is quite different from our modern term symmetry (bi-lateral symmetry).
We cannot do better than to give the definition of Vitruvius:
"Symmetry resides in the correlation by measurement between the various elements of the plan, and between each of these elements and the whole…. As in the human body…it proceeds from pro-portion—the proportion the Greeks called *analogia*—and achieves consonance between every part and the whole…. When every important part of the building is thus conveniently set in proportion by the right correlation between height and width, between width and depth, and when all these parts also have their place in the total symmetry of the building, we obtain eurhythmy."

The final line of the text is separated out, creating both an effective emphasis and a linear bridge to the abstract elements.

**Features:**
Two sizes of dots, quantity
variable. Numerals
augment the dot structure
as part of the interpretive
language.

grid

**Expansion on Text 8:**
The expansion set permits
variable dot size and
variable placement of all
elements. The set shows
alternatives in dynamic
symmetry to reinforce the
text's stress on integration
as compared to bilateral
symmetry.

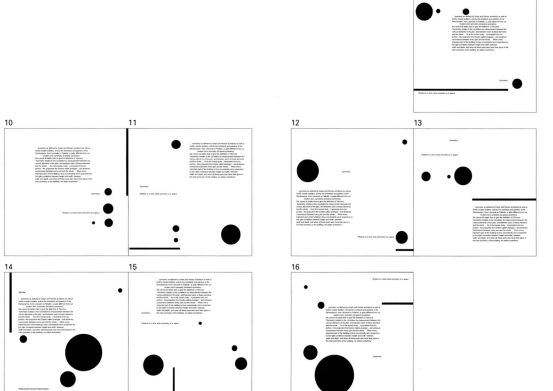

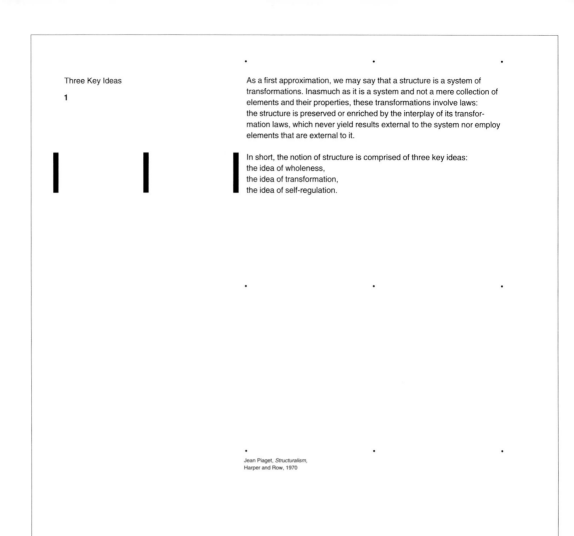

Three Key Ideas

**1**

As a first approximation, we may say that a structure is a system of transformations. Inasmuch as it is a system and not a mere collection of elements and their properties, these transformations involve laws: the structure is preserved or enriched by the interplay of its transformation laws, which never yield results external to the system nor employ elements that are external to it.

In short, the notion of structure is comprised of three key ideas: the idea of wholeness, the idea of transformation, the idea of self-regulation.

Jean Piaget, *Structuralism*, Harper and Row, 1970

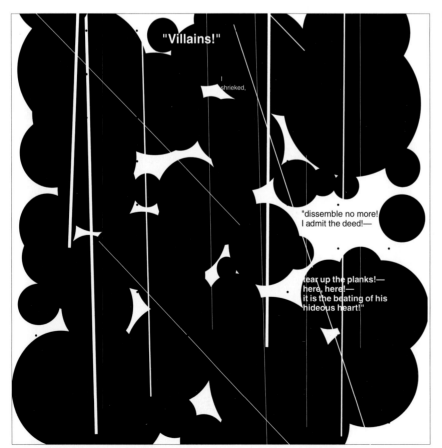

**Features:**
Dot and line grids in variable weight and interstices are used to reinforce the meaning and structure of the texts.

**Replacement Text:**
A horror subject by Edgar Allen Poe is the basis for an expansion on the formal language of the first set.

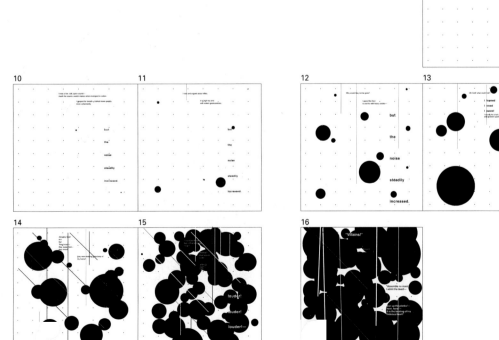

Spoken and Written

Language and writing are two different systems of signs;
the only purpose of the latter is to represent the former.
Linguistics is not concerned
with the connection between the written and spoken word—
its sole object is the latter: the spoken word.
~~But the written word is so closely bound up with the spoken, whose image it is,~~
~~that it is increasingly arrogating the main role to itself.~~
~~Ultimately the point is reached~~
~~where more importance is attached to representation of the spoken sign~~
~~than to this sign itself.~~
It's like thinking that to know someone,
~~it is better to look at his photograph than his face.~~

*5*

■ Ferdinand de Saussure, "Cours de linguistique générale,"
Bally and Sechehaye, Lausanne, 1916

that it is increasingly arrogating the main role to itself.

spoken

Ultimately the point is reached

w ritten

where more importance is attached to representation of the spoken sign

Language

than to the sign itself.

**Features:**
Numerals advance within a tight zone while a square of constant size shifts position across the whole format.

grid

1

2

3

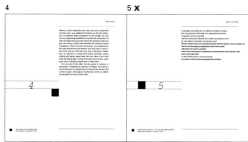

4

5 **x**

6

7

8

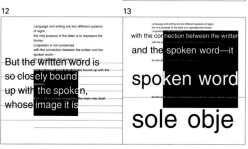

**Expansion on Text 5:**
The strike-through feature is amplified. The written text reaches an ascendancy, then loses it to the spoken.

9

10

11

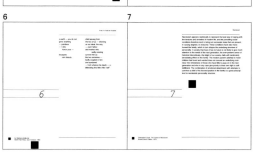

12

13

14

15

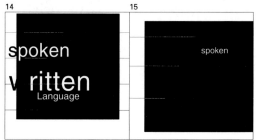

16

4 enlargement

When you have forded the river, when you have crossed the mountain pass, you suddenly find before you the city of Moriana, its alabaster gates transparent in the sunlight, its coral columns supporting pediments encrusted with serpentine, its villas all of glass like aquariums where the shadows of dancing girls with silvery scales swim beneath the medusa-shaped chandeliers. If this is not your first journey, you already know that cities like this have an obverse: you have only to walk in a semicircle and you will come into view of Moriana's hidden face, an expanse of rusting sheet metal, sackcloth, planks bristling with spikes, pipes black with soot, piles of tins, blind walls with fading signs, frames of staved-in straw chairs, ropes good only for hanging oneself from a rotten beam.

From one part to the other, the city seems to continue, in perspective, multiplying its repertory of images: but instead it has no thickness, it consists only of a face and an obverse, like a sheet of paper, with a figure on either side, which can neither be separated nor look at each other.

4    **Cities and Eyes**

Italo Calvino, from *Invisible Cities*,
Harcourt Brace Jovanovich, 1974

10, 11 enlargements

**She said:**
It's

# hard.
### hard.

It's just kind of
**hard**
to say.

He said:

Isn't it. Isn't it just. Isn't it just like a woman.

**She said:** *It  goes.*

It goes that way.

## *That's the way it*

# *goes.*

**Features:**
Overlapping rectangles of 2 screen values relate simultaneously to the shape of the text and its content.

grid

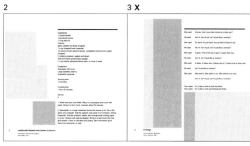

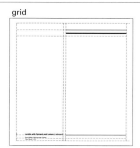

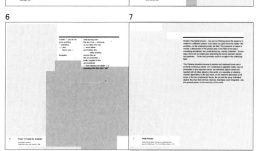

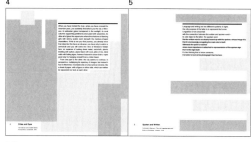

**Expansion on Text 3:**
Variation in type size, weight, slant, and placement is used to stress the contrast between male and female voices in the "IT Tango."

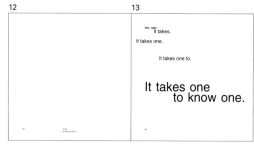

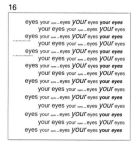

10
She said:
It's
# hard.
hard.
It's just kind of **hard** to say.

11
She said: *It goes.*
It goes that way.
# *That's the way it*
# *goes.*

12

13
She said: It takes.
It takes one.
It takes one to.
It takes one to know one.

14

15
She said:
She said it. She said it to me. She said it to me one.

16
eyes your eyes eyes *your* eyes **your** eyes
your eyes your eyes *your* eyes
eyes your eyes eyes *your* eyes **your eyes**
your eyes your eyes *your* eyes
eyes your eyes eyes *your* eyes **your eyes**
your eyes your eyes *your* eyes
eyes your eyes eyes *your* eyes **your** eyes
your eyes your eyes *your* eyes
eyes your eyes eyes *your* eyes **your eyes**
your eyes your eyes *your* eyes
eyes your eyes eyes *your* eyes **your** eyes
your eyes your eyes *your* eyes
eyes your eyes eyes *your* eyes **your eyes**

Forms with a clear
counterpoint of space tend
to maintain clarity and
expand the sense of space
when they are mixed.

o earth — you do not
grow anything
— pointless
— I who
    honor you —

bouquets
    vain beauty

child sprung from
the two of us — showing
us our ideal, the way
— ours! father
and mother who
        sadly existing
survive him as
the two extremes —
badly coupled in him
and sundered
— from whence his death — o-
bliterating this little child "self"

❺

She said:     It looks. Don't you think it looks a lot like rain?

He said:     Isn't it. Isn't it just. Isn't it just like a woman?

She said:     It's hard. It's just hard. It's just kind of hard to say.

He said:     Isn't it. Isn't it just. Isn't it just like a woman?

She said:     It goes. That's the way it goes. It goes that way.

He said:     Isn't it. Isn't it just like a woman?

She said:     It takes. It takes one. It takes one to. It takes one to know

He said:     Isn't it just like a woman?

She said:     She said it. She said it to no. She said it to no one.

**1.**

Isn't it. Isn't it just. Isn't it just like a woman?

Wash and pick over lentils. Place in a saucepan and cover with
water. Bring to a boil. Cook, covered, about 20 minutes.

❹     Statements by Walter Thirring and Joseph Needham,
     quoted in Fritjof Kapra, *The Tao of Physics*, Bantam, 1975

Your eyes:     It's a day's work to look into them.
Your eyes:     It's a day's work just looking into them.

Lemon

Field Force

essence of
isible—the
matter is
lace;
sh." Accord
n elemen-
underlying

al times was a
pable matter was not
dual objects acted and
world...in a wavelike or vibratory
manner dependent, in the last resort, on the rhythmic alternation at all
levels of the two fundamental forces, the *yin* and the *yang*. Individual
objects thus had their intrinsic rhythm     nd these were integrated...into
the general pattern of the     world.

Spoken :

Language and writing are two different systems of signs;
the only purpose of the latter is to represent the former.
Linguistics is not concerned
with the connection between the written and spoken word—
its sole object is the latter: the spoken word.
But the written word is so closely bound up with the spoken, wh
that it is increasingly arrogating the main role to itself.
Ultimately the point is reached
where more importance is attached to representation of the spo
than to this sign itself.

**o n i o n s**
**o l i v e   o i l g a r l i c**
f r e s h l y   g r o u n d   p e p p e r

s

# 2.

*The alphabet is a logical and convenient base for sign-symbols. Participants in a summer session apply a catalog of letter variation options (morphology) to a set of three letters to develop a sign-symbol identity for the session itself. The letters CM–B derive from Carnegie Mellon (University) and Basel (Switzerland), the alternating host locations. In the expansion phase, a poster motif is developed.*

The examples on pages 58–59 and 62–63 are by participants in the program *Graphic Design, Typography and the Computer,* Carnegie-Mellon University. All other documentation and examples by the author.

• **Technical Notes:**
Illustrator 88® was used for most of the drawings on pages 50–59 and 62–63. Aldus FreeHand® was used for most of the drawings in the expansion series. Encapsulated postscript files were placed in PageMaker® and resized as necessary to adjust to the grid.

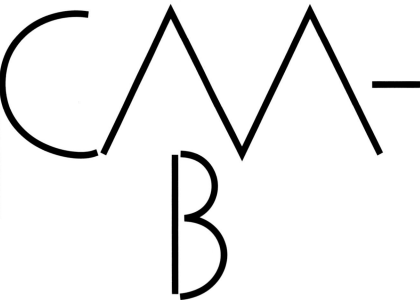

**Logical Goal:**
To understand the variation and meaning potential of the letter configuration CM-B through visual research.

**Personal Goal:**
To engage in a process of intelligent play yielding a form which feels right, is more than logical, more than cause and effect.

**Pragmatic Goal:**
To develop a visual mark for a summer program linking Carnegie Mellon University and faculty of the Basel (Switzerland) School of Design. The program establishes a dynamic relationship between classical design methods and computer-assisted methods.

**Process:**

**1**
Analyze letter components.
**2**
Explore possibilities for formal variation based on a furnished morphology—which describes structural changes in a systematic way—and intuitive search. Limit parameters to 1.1–1.6 from morphology.
**3**
Apply multiple parameters and combinations.
**4**
Interpret formal qualities in terms of meaning.
**5**
Focus on one form as a new beginning point for further development and nuance.
**6**
Expand the limits of the final form to yield a poster motif; reapply the morphology.

The CM-B Base

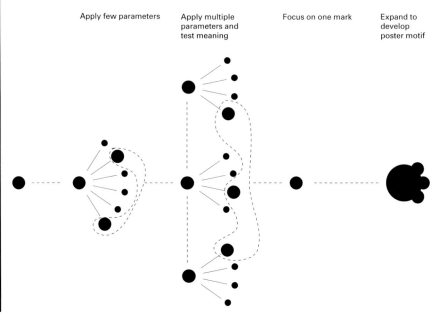

Apply few parameters

Apply multiple parameters and test meaning

Focus on one mark

Expand to develop poster motif

Notes concerning studio procedure:

•
Visual research means trying out visual alternatives. Speculation is not enough; alternatives have to be seen.

•
Criteria become clearer as visual forms evolve. This minimizes second-guessing and preconceiving solutions.

•
Overloading of inert information, that is, information that is not useful to the project at hand, is avoided. The assumption is that only information that is applied is retained.

•
Logical file management and identification of each step are essential when alternatives are generated on the computer. The process of ordering alternatives involves naming; naming involves focusing a quality and culling out redundancy. This is an essential part of design.

•
Learning to use the fewest possible control points to create a form in a computer drawing program is an important first discipline.

•
The process outline is linear for convenience and initial clarity. However, the morphology suggests lateral movement and another vantage point. It serves both staying within and jumping outside a system.

### Letter Width and Geometry

The base configuration of the letters CM-B, which is the beginning point for this project, can be thought of as an armature to be "fleshed out." The letter forms are governed by the principle of variable letter widths. The alphabet can be seen as structured in two basically different ways. In the classic Roman form, letter width is defined in relation to the square.

Wider forms (left), based on a full square, are contrasted with typically narrower forms (right) based on a half square. The contrast between narrow and wide letters gives the alphabet a liveliness which needs to be calmed by consistent and generous optical spacing. In the second example, the three letters in Univers (left, an equal width system), Times Roman (center, a variable width system), and a simplified and exaggerated variable width system (right) are compared.

We can separate the B into two parts and provide another element to work with. This also improves the rhythmic potential though too great a separation could cause confusion with the number 13.

When forms are perfectly round, they don't look round; when perfectly square, they don't look square. Quality in a visual image involves the adjustment of geometry for the way the tandem human optical system, placed on a horizontal axis, perceives.

The history of letter forms shows that sensitivity to the vertical-horizontal differential has characterized all great letter-form design. This requires an optical center higher than the geometric center, and a horizontal stroke weaker in relation to the vertical stroke. (This characteristic persists through present-day typeface design, but it is jeopardized by the ability to easily distort letter proportion using the computer.) The CM-B armature respects the shift of optical center, but its weight is undifferentiated because the weight will be redefined as the form is built up. By assigning this simplified, linear form, a more universal and neutral beginning point is established.

Training to observe optically true geometric forms is like learning to tune an instrument, or to create nuances of flavor in cooking. You make the adjustment enough times until you feel it.

In this row of H-forms, the outer two are useless exaggerations and the third has a mathematically centered crossbar. The second shows the effect of adjustment to reflect the need for optical balance.

Try this: make a series of variations on the square to determine which version feels wider or narrower than a square with equal sides. The version felt not to be wider than it is high is a perceptually correct square.

Which is the perceptually true square in this row, which the geometric? The most convincing square is probably number 3, but number 4 is the geometrically true one. (This test should be done with larger elements for a more reliable and refined result. Only two adjacent forms at a time should be compared.)

M O Q T X   B P R S

**CMB**  CMB  CMB

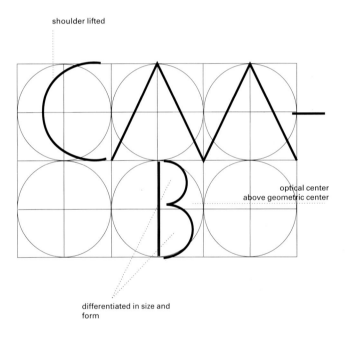

shoulder lifted

optical center
above geometric center

differentiated in size and
form

H H H H

1   2   3   4   5   6   7

etc.

> *". . . a single message is of interest only from the point of view of its relationship with all other messages which could have been sent but were not."*
> **—Claude Shannon**

### Formal Analysis

In the CM-B project, the given information deals with underlying systems of letter proportion, a method of analysis, and a morphological framework. We avoid studying finished styles, which may be considered external information. Rather than adding to existing style, the letter forms are first broken down to more basic units. This has the effect of revealing the inner structure of the letters and releasing new energy. (Sifting out the subsets opens the way for fresh possibilities in animation as well.)

Analysis reveals that any given part belongs to more than one subset. Including each element in several subsets simultaneously gives the apparently simple total form an unexpected dynamic and richness.

The knowledge of a form in its essential makeup is the basis for experimentation. It invites looking at the sets as beginning points, as stress or emphasis points, as a challenge to the imagination, and as a purging of the temptations to appropriate finished or clichéd styles.

The inventory of subsets includes spaces, placed on an equal footing with the positive forms. The simultaneous expression of form and space as one congruous whole, not as foreground and background, gives the simplest form a vibrancy and presence. It is not necessary to rely on serifs or other details to relieve the monotony of the simple form, as is often felt. The use of any such elements should be a function of expression rather than decoration.

Being objective at the beginning of an exploration gives us a measure of confidence that we can delete stifling forms to which we're perhaps attached, but which interfere with a new, emerging expression. Analyzing the parts sets the stage for objectivity because it takes off the pressure to immediately find a solution.

The tension between distinct parts and the harmonious whole is the classic organizational problem. Successfully resolving the conflict between those aspects consists in finding a resonant flux between parts and whole, the goal and criterion for most visual forms.

The kind of whole that commandeers the parts so that they forfeit their individual expression is a tyrant. When the parts detract from the image of the whole, anarchy results.

### Structure

### Deconstruction

rounds

repeating forms

straights

narrow-width forms

right diagonals

right angle

mid-zone

convergences

anchor points

bilateral symmetry

large spaces

analogous spaces

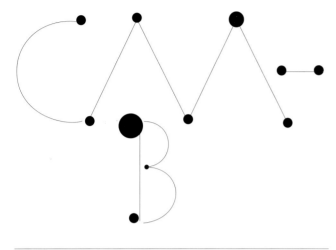

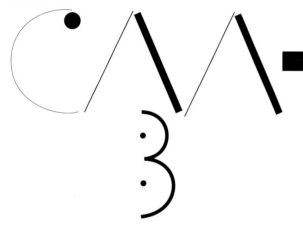

In the rush to make a recognizable image, an easily acceptable image for quick consumption, clarity of the parts is often sacrificed. In human terms, something gets trampled on.

A parts analysis is not a way to solve the problem; it is a way to gain access to it, to open it, to lay it bare.

A parts analysis reveals aspects of the form not immediately seen and suggests useful features or points of departure for investigation. Parts are brought into motion in a dynamic relationship; motion is the basis for emotion; an emotional response in turn is the basis for memorability. If memorability is a goal, then it's desirable to have a certain degree of disorienting action which disturbs the clichéd and predictable. If we strategically place the elements used to create accents within the CM-B configuration, as shown in the hybrid sifts at left, legibility can improve at the same time that interest is increased.

Of course, an idea must be projected, and the parts structure needs to serve the idea. The analysis itself does not produce ideas, but it can set the stage for new ideas that originate in the form itself.

If a sense of movement, differentiation, and experimentation are conveyed, we are already on the way toward an appropriate form for the stated purpose.

**"Perhaps the most basic thing that can be said about human memory, after a century of intensive research, is that unless detail is placed into a structured pattern, it is rapidly forgotten."**
**—Jerome Bruner**

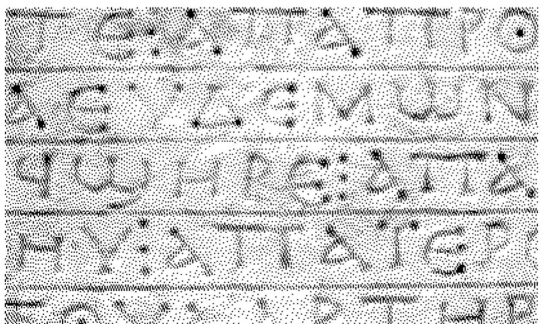

A Greek stone inscription with accented stress points emphasizes letter features for legibility and overall texture.

### Morphology, Norms, and the Contrast Continuum

Limiting the options often spawns a unique quality; creativity is most apparent when limitation is used inventively. In learning, the awareness of the range of possibilities must be balanced by exploration of the potential expressive range within *one* possibility. A morphology, a system for defining how type can be varied, gives the designer an overview of possibilities. It also helps reduce confusion because very often we are using more options at once than we realize. Developing only one at a time to its fullest potential is therefore an important preparatory discipline.

We live in a world of disappearing norms, yet clear points of reference are necessary for communication. Effective communication both surprises and assures. The stronger the sense and focus of the normative, the clearer the sense of the exception. Conversely, the more the exceptions, the more obscure the message. A complex, texturally rich, information-poor statement will tend to feel appropriate in an environment of proliferation; it may therefore be interesting without being clear, but it may not be at all effective for the intended communication.

If reliance on broadly understood norms is not possible, the designer must know how structure helps to create a base for understanding. Then a meaningful exception can be made to complete the communication. Thus, if all letters are the same size except one, both the norm and the exception are visibly created. No other normative criterion is required.

A contrast continuum is a useful tool for placing a norm in context. It describes the range possible within one parameter. It is usually possible to locate where on the continuum the norm will fall. A sense of extremes, besides helping to clarify the norm, gives important clues for the exaggeration of contrast necessary for communication. The opposite poles of the continuum should not be thought of as having inherently positive or negative connotations. Any appropriate attribute can be useful. The ranges and definition of normal, when applicable, are shown in relation to the individual options in the morphology.

Once it is made distinct, contrast will *inherently* tend to create a meaning structure. It alerts us to a change within which we seek meaning. Finding a contrasting form is a way, therefore, of triggering meaning without the burden, at first, of solving a problem. Paradoxically, the problem is often more interestingly and genuinely addressed when the pressure of the "problem" is lifted.

Morphologies can be used as a source of rules or limitations by which a new form is experienced. In an ideal state these qualities will be quite definitely distinguishable. When applied and brought to bear on specific content, the ultimate complexity of relationships will tend to blur the original clear distinctions. Consequently more complex forms will be seen differently by different persons, and more and more different things will be seen by the same person. For this reason, the tables showing the application of a given morphology, especially as these are applied to more complex subjects later in this chapter (but also elsewhere in this book), should not be thought of as an *absolute* listing of attributes. Rather they are ones that the author perceived at a certain time. For the readers this can only be interesting as a comparison to how they might themselves react. If one sees it differently, the process of trying to figure out why someone else saw it another way could be a useful exercise in seeing. What this points out is that any integration of characteristics is more than the sum of its parts. It is also true that, although using a morphology may clarify an investigation, its use is no guarantee of the quality of a visual form. To avoid confusion, explore each option exclusive of the others before any are mixed; and in mixing, combine no more than two qualities in one image at first.

Practice with using a morphological matrix embeds the range of formal possibilities in the mind. With training in using each quality separately and effectively, the designer is free to function in a more creative role as synthesizer.

Valuable advice on choosing a guitar came in words something like this:

If you listen to many guitars in succession, you will tend to find a good quality in each one. Your dilemma increases with each new instrument added to the array. Your decision, besides being difficult, is often wrong, based on superficiality.

If you compare two instruments at a time, it is far less difficult to decide which of the two is superior. By making a succession of comparisons in this way, it is possible to work through an array of choices with much greater assurance and clarity that the final choice is a good one.

This technique is extremely useful, not only for shopping, but any situation where the number of choices is overwhelming.
—kh

Contrast continuum showing norm (**N**) when applicable.
For some categories, no norm applies. In these
cases, the change is a formal choice in which the effect
on legibility is judged on a case-by-case basis.

**1.  Letter Form:**

Range applied to CM-B base

| | |
|---|---|
| equal **N** ........................................................ disparate <br><br> Disparate size breaks the continuity of relationship. | **1.1 size** |
| geometric ...................... **N** .................... eccentric <br><br> Geometric and eccentric are both stylistic extremes, but the norm is more geometric than eccentric. Geometric is static; eccentric needs to support the content. | **1.2 face** |
| light ...................... **N** ...................... heavy <br><br> Both light and heavy are extremes, but the norm is not exactly in the middle; it is closer to light, confirming that the eye picks up greater nuance of change at lighter values. | **1.3 weight** |
| condensed ................................ **N** .......... expanded <br><br> A letter can be condensed more extremely than it can be expanded. While condensed letters can be elegant, expanded ones often appear stretched out of shape. Changes in width require adjustments to the treatment of curves. | **1.4 width** |
| vertical ............ **13–16°** ............... diagonal <br><br> Vertical (roman) is the norm for type and most constructed letters; slanted is the norm for handwriting; 13–16° is the normal range for italic. | **1.5 slant** |
| lower ............ **N1** ................ **N2** upper <br><br> Mixed upper and lower is the norm (N1) for text legibility; upper case is the norm (N2) for symbols. | **1.6 case** |
| | **1.7 other** <br><br> **1.8 combinations** |

For every category, it is assumed that other qualities may be discovered and that combinations of features may be applied.

| Contrast continuum showing norm (N) when applicable | 2. Letter Alterations<br>3. Letter Arrangement | Applied to CM-B base |
|---|---|---|
| joined **N** ...................................................... separated<br><br>While the complete letter is normative, it is not necessarily more legible than a skillful fragmentation. | **2.1**<br>**connection** | |
| abstract ...................................................... metaphor<br><br>Substitution, creating visual puns, is enticing and also difficult because it is easy to lose a formal relationship. | **2.2**<br>**substitution** | |
| integral ...................................................... mutilated<br><br>Integral distortion preserves and accentuates essential letter identity; mutilation destroys it. Both can be useful. | **2.3**<br>**distortion** | |
| flat **N** ...................................................... deep<br><br>The flat image is normal for a flat surface. A dimensional image is illusionary and signals a new meaning. | **2.4**<br>**depth** | |
| overlapping **N** ...................................................... isolated<br><br>Normal letter spacing allows one to sense the word, neither crowded nor loose. If pushed to one of the extremes, it should be for a formal or expressive reason. | **3.1**<br>**spacing** | |
| single **N** ...................................................... many<br><br>Repetition produces redundancy which might be effective or might reduce the image to ornamentation instead of communication. The ease of creating repetition with the computer encourages the substitution of decoration for design. | **3.2**<br>**repetition** | |
| casual ...................................................... chaotic<br><br>Is the distribution of letters a controlled event, a semi-random construct, or purely the result of a chance operation? | **3.3**<br>**randomness** | |

Contrast continuum (norms not applicable)

Applied to CM-B base

fixed .............................................................. variable

**4.1
rule lines**

Rules are useful for defining position on the page or amplifying the letter structure. Rule lines easily produce a graphic look without substance.

as is .......................................................... constructed

**4.2
typographic
elements**

Punctuation and other symbolic marks from typographic fonts tend to maintain their integrity of language when inserted into a letter structure.

free ............................................................ mechanical

**4.3
drawings**

Drawing is the most difficult element to combine with a letter structure; it requires a clear translation into a formal vocabulary for a convincing relationship to be created.

tonal ........................................................... translated

**4.4
photo-
graphs**

The digitization of photographs, whether by a conventional halftone process or the application of other conversion techniques, often has an inherent advantage over drawing in relating to constructed forms because of the mechanical consistency.

analogous ...................................................... opposing

**4.5
shape**

Adding a shape to a letter configuration can result in framing, in which case the redundancy might weaken the image, or result in an opposing shape, which will tend to strengthen the image.

For every category, it is assumed that other qualities may be discovered and that combinations of features may be applied.

Shown are selections from a sketch process used by Richard Woollacott to arrive at his solution, one of the twelve solutions, pages 62–63. The exploration gradually assumed a focus on letter distortion.

The process yields potential which may be inappropriate for the requirements of a sign-symbol, but which can be useful for other applications.

In the expansion phase some of the nascent qualities of the search emerge again in more clearly defined form.

1.2 face
1.3 weight
2.3 distortion          +   1.1 size                    3.2 repetition              combinations

simplification by
concentrating
on amorphous forms

further simplification ;
controlling amorphous
forms to represent letter
forms

composite resolution

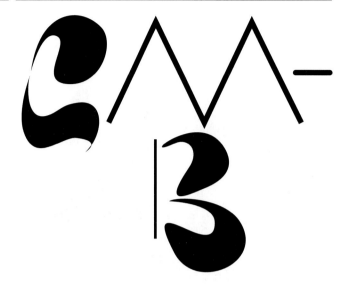

**Sample Expansion**

In the expansion phase, the sign-symbol is a fresh beginning point for development of a poster motif. The morphology is re-applied.

additional features or changes applied:
1.3 weight (screen tints)
3.2 repetition
3.3 randomness
4.6 other, custom elements added

Abstract shapes generated in the first stage are used as an environment for the sign-symbol. These could serve as basic poster motifs around which information would be structured.

additional features or
changes applied:
1.1 size, of parts
3.1 spacing, overlap
2.2 substitution of pattern

The amorphous shapes are
exaggerated and combined
into one. The resulting
concentration yields a
more dynamic poster idea.

General criteria as evolved by working alternately from morphology and intuition while preserving an essential quality of the base configuration:

•

The CM-B summer program is characterized by a playful search for new expression. Suggestions of digitization, of the synaptic, of the open-ended, the unknown, the unpredictable, of fresh beginnings are appropriate.

•

The use of the computer is offset by conventional and intuitive hand/ perceptual processes.

•

Visual exploration is the central dynamic idea.

Solutions by:
Walter Bohatsch
J. Anne Cornell
Alyce Nadine Hoggan
Amy Pfeiffer

Terry Swack
Crit G. Warren
Jennifer Mumford
Richard Woollacott

Betsy Kurzinger
Christopher E. Lozos
Cynthia S. Malon
Celia Metcalf

**1**
1.2 face
1.3 weight
2.2 substitution
3.3 randomness
4.1 rule lines

Stars-and-stripes/Swiss cross connotation at one level; matrix as meshing point between two poles on another level.

**2**
1.4 width
2.2 substitution
4.2 typographic elements

Reciprocating C and B with compressed, elastic M and dots as dynamic link.

**3**
1.1 size
1.3 weight (color)
4.2 typographic elements

Composite, continuous large form countered by scattered, free, small forms gives a connotation of individual freedom within a substantial program.

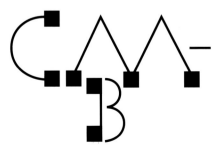

**4**
4.2 typographic elements

The elements suggest serifs but are strong enough as geometry to suggest an additional, separate playful quality.

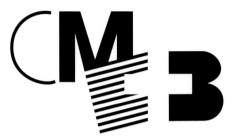

**5**
1.2  face
1.3  weight
2.2  substitution
4.5  shape

The filled letters set up a context for cutting away—structuring, de-structuring.

**9**
1.3  weight
3.3  randomness
4.2  typographic elements

Opposing elements dance in a free array of raw material.

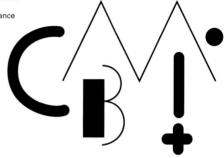

**6**
1.1  size
1.2  face
1.3  weight
4.2  typographic elements

A free spatial organization suggests probing. The dash element assumes a new role as stabilizer for each of the three letters and the whole composition.

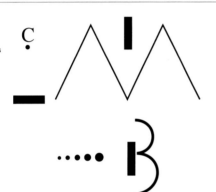

**10**
1.1  size
2.2  substitution
2.4  depth
4.2  typographic elements

Flag references are simultaneously basic form references.

**7**
1.1  size
1.3  weight
1.4  width
2.2  substitution
4.5  shape

Against an enclosure, the elements are pushing out, varying, exploring.

**11**
1.3  weight
1.4  width
1.5  slant
2.4  depth

Letter parts become signs in space.

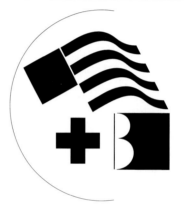

**8**
1.3  weight
2.3  distortion

Curvilinear segments are emphasized as organic, reciprocal shapes. The tension is between the human and the mechanistic.

**12**
1.3  weight
1.6  case
2.2  substitution
3.3  randomness
4.5  shape

The linking dash becomes a focal point within a differentiated grouping.

additional features or
changes applied:
1.1  size
4.6  other, coarse screen

The extreme scale change
and application of a dot
grid convey a sense of
location and concentrate
the movement.

additional features or
changes applied:
3.2  repetition, part
4.2  typographic elements

The scattered quality of the
original logo, in itself a
questionable quality in a
logo, gains by repetition
and exaggeration.

Two variations on the same base show the radically different effect of different groups of features.

Below:
additional features or changes applied:
1.1  size
3.1  spacing, overlap
3.2  repetition, single
4.6  other, positive/
      negative shift

Enlarging the more abstract elements emphasizes the visual.

Right:
additional features or changes applied:
1.1  size
4.3  drawing

The enlarged *B* becomes an arena for the contrast of exploratory and refined forms.

additional features or
changes applied:
1.1 size
1.3 weight
3.2 repetition, part
4.5 shape
4.6 other, rotation

A centrifugal motion is
combined with an aperture
image to express opening
and enlargement of vision.

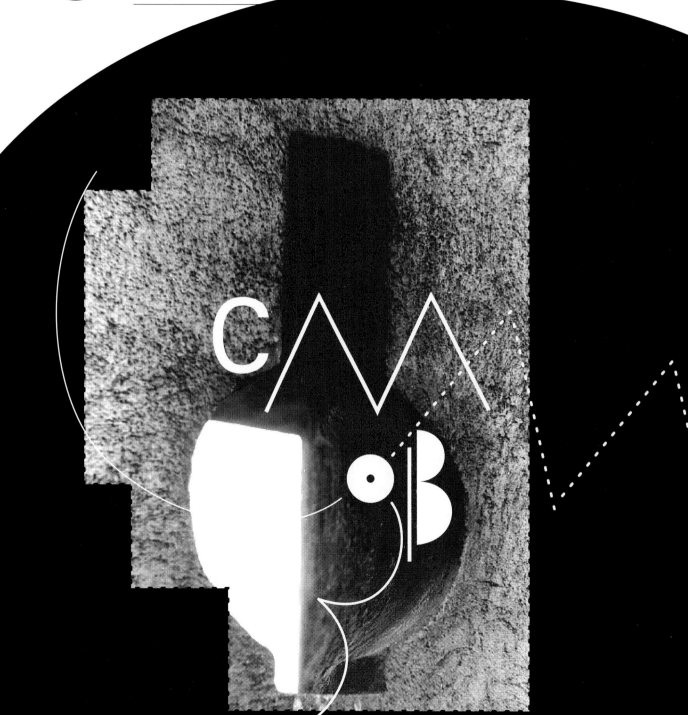

additional features or
changes applied:
1.1   size
3.1   spacing, overlap
3.2   repetition

The compounding of the
triple dot motif creates an
environment of surprising
depth and complexity.

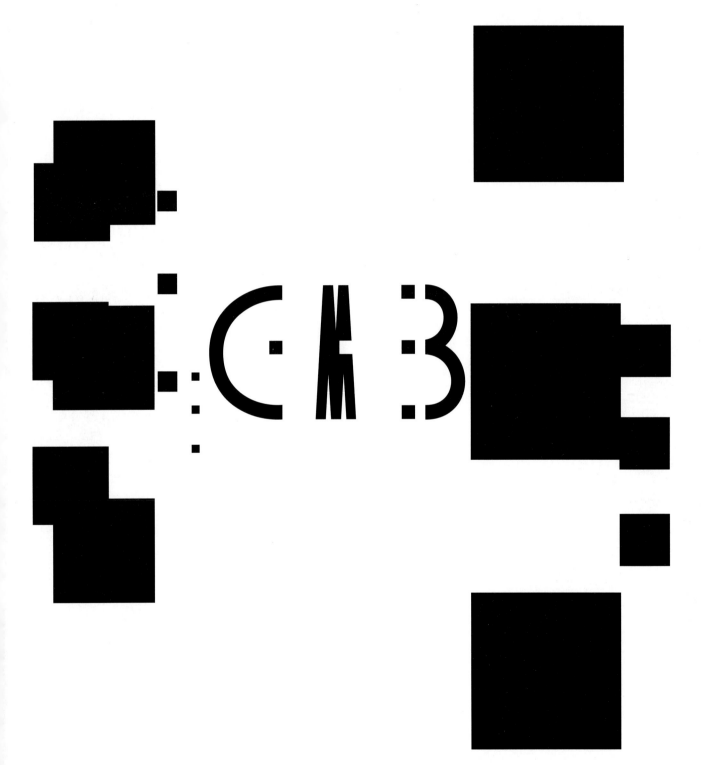

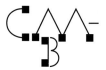

additional features or
changes applied:
2.2   substitution

(expansion version
by Amy Pfeiffer)

Altering the termination
points of strokes suggests
new connections being
made.

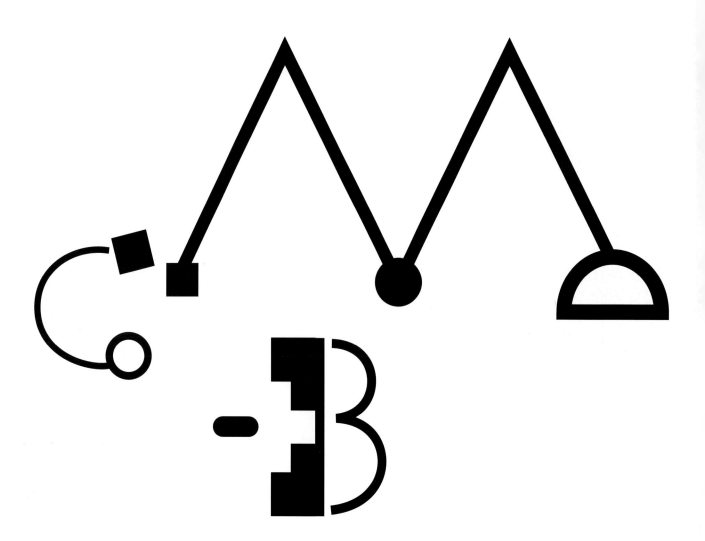

additional features or
changes applied:
1.1  size
2.4  depth
4.1  rule lines
4.5  shape
4.6  other, tonal gradation

A delicate logo is given
an environment of
boldness that echoes its
spatial connotations.

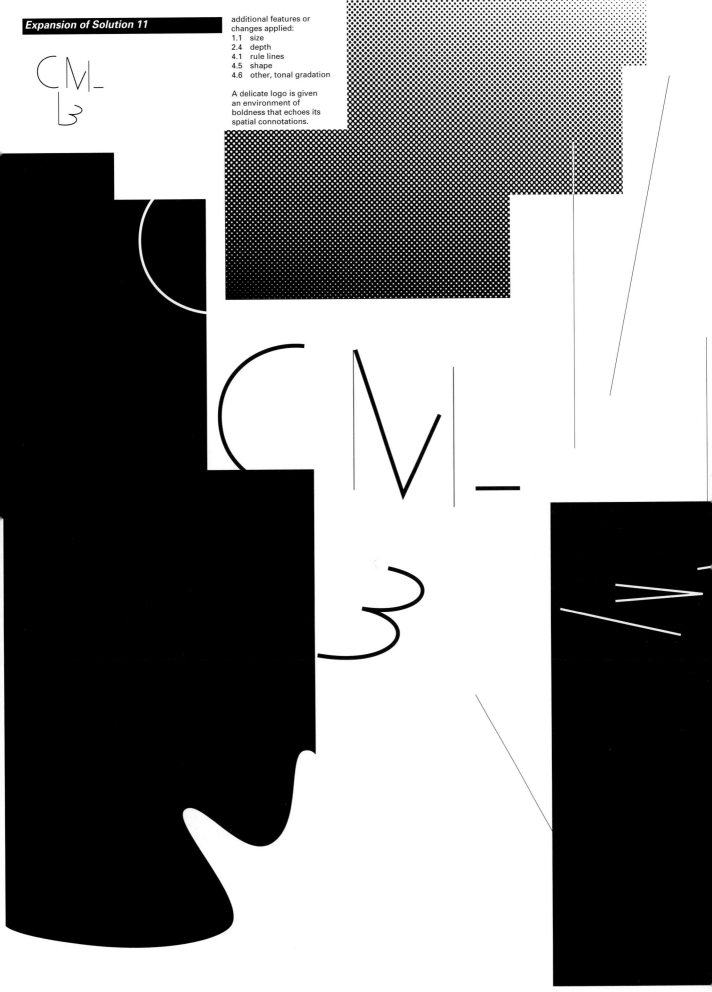

Two variations on the same base show the radically different effect of different groups of features.

Below:
additional features or changes applied:
3.2   repetition
4.1   rule lines
4.4   photographs
4.5   shape

The digitization of Basel's historical setting represents the tension created by the new technology.

Right:
additional features or changes applied:
1.1   size
1.3   weight
2.3   distortion
4.3   drawing

A loosening up of the flag elements conveys openness and vitality.

additional features or
changes applied:
4.1  rule lines
4.5  shape
4.6  other, pattern, tiles

Letter forms, pushing out
from the edges, are
released as rhythmic
abstractions.

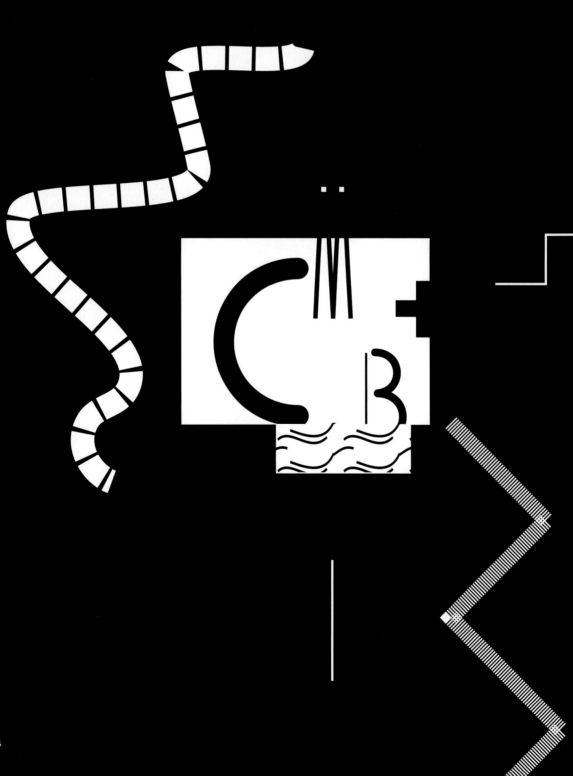

additional features or
changes applied:
3.2   repetition, part
3.3   randomness

By simple repetition,
the hyphen expresses the
surge of process and the
excitement of the
unknown.

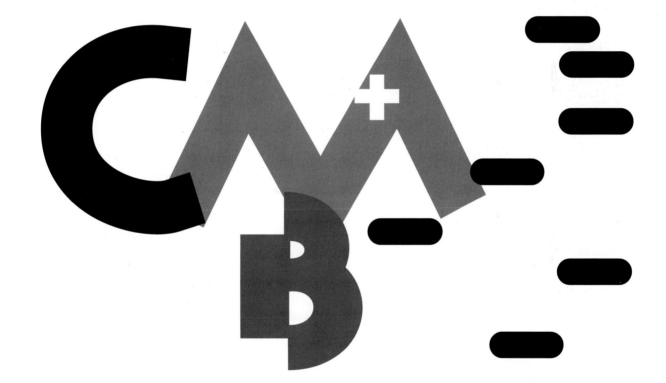

additional features or
changes applied:
3.2   repetition
3.3   randomness
4.4   photographs

The search for the new is
in the physical context of
the old.

# 3.

*Words can function as captions, labels, or integrated elements in relation to picture images. The integration of words and images, a classic problem for the graphic designer, is the focus of this project.*

*A program is explored for building a set of variations on a three-word text in combination with a separate set of photographic and videographic images of the cup.*

All examples are by the author.

**• Technical Notes:**
An 8mm video camera with macro setting and MacVision® software was used to scan the images on pages 84–86, 89, 95–102, as 8-bit gray scale TIFF images. The remaining pages contain photographs scanned in an 8-bit scanner. Further adjustment of brightness, contrast, edge definition, and local correction was done in Digital Darkroom®. Final placement, screen frequency, and angle were defined in the print documents which were prepared in Aldus FreeHand®. The Linotronic output was at 2540 dpi.

**Personal Goals:**

*To engage in a free-spirited investigation of the possibilities for formal relationship between word and visual image.*

*To observe the effect of aspects of formal relationship in creating either a supportive or subversive interaction of word and picture image.*

*To explore the potential for a simple, more neutral typeface to assume many different expressive roles from lightness and fragility to clumsiness and brutality as size, spacing, tonality, and configuration are explored.*

*To develop a useful and simple morphology to describe and clarify the interactions in a broad sense.*

*To use digital scans of photographs and a video camera with low-end digital image processing software to produce the picture images.*

*To use a digital drawing program to manipulate and integrate typographic and picture images.*

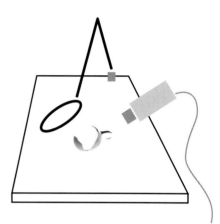

**Process:**

**1**
*Define subject.*
An ordinary but interesting object is chosen.

**2**
*Use preliminary video scans to get a feel for the subject.*
An 8mm video camera and single light source are used in a table-top set-up; MacVision® is the digitizing program. (See photo on page 202.)

**3**
*Define type limitations.*
The Univers family—a universal typeface useful for a wide range of transformations with minimal loss of legibility—is selected as the base.

**4**
*Define a base format.*
Unless there are other restrictions, the square is the most basic and universal format, against which image dynamics are most effectively contrasted.

**5**
*Explore effects of screen frequency (dots per inch), dot shape and screen angle on image quality from an expressive viewpoint.*
(As permitted by the program Aldus Freehand®: 8–150 lines per inch; round, square, or elliptical dot structure; any screen angle.)

**6.**
*Explore effects of transformational tools on image quality.*
These include overall and local changes in contrast, brightness, positive–negative relationship, dithering, and others offered by MacVision®, Digital Darkroom®, and FreeHand®.

**7**
*Combine image and type intuitively.*
These are sessions to explore a range of possibilities and to test word legibility in the visual context.

**8**
*Sort and classify the results according to the morphology. Revise the morphology as necessary.*

**9**
*Use the morphology to clarify confusing relationships, to show other possibilities and to eliminate redundancy.*
The morphology is explained on pages 80–81.

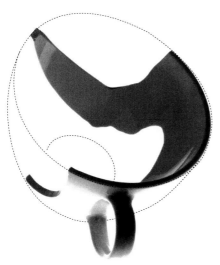

One day I fumbled a purportedly unbreakable cup on the
kitchen counter. It fell, perhaps eight inches, into the vinyl
coated basket of the dishwasher—and broke in several
pieces. The unusual form of the biggest fragment began to
intrigue me, and over the years I have returned to it as a
thing to study. It is the relationship between the pristine
regularity and finish of the original cup design and the
aggressive, amorphous break that creates tension and
interest. By coupling the advertised quality of the cup
with its demise, an ironic base situation is established.
That a cup with such profoundly durable qualities should
have not just chipped, but shattered in a relatively gentle
fall, demonstrates the vulnerability of all apparently strong
things to freak stresses that can destroy them.

The challenge to me was to use this broken state to create
alternately the expression of this vulnerability and a new,
restorative wholeness by means of visual composition,
light and shadow, and through combination with type.

## THE UNBREAKABLE
# cup

**The Basic Elements**

Throughout the examples,
the *c* and *p* of the word *cup*
and the handle are
the basis for analogous,
recursive form.

| | | | |
|---|---|---|---|
| content: verbal/visual | **V** | / | ☜ |
| scale: subordinate/dominant | · | / | ● |
| grouping of elements: regular/irregular | ⸬ | / | ⁙ |
| dimensionality: flat/spatial | ☐ | / | ❏ |
| message quality: informational/expressive | **i** | / | ⚇ |

**Words**, as distinct from pictures, are summarized as being:
- verbal
- subordinate in size
- regular and left-to-right in configuration
- spatially flat
- primarily informational

**Pictures**, as distinct from words, are summarized as being:
- visual
- dominant in scale
- irregular or at least not linearly sequential in arrangement of the elements
- three-dimensionally spatial
- primarily expressive and emotional in character

## Morphology

The basic ideas of contrast governing the relationships between words and pictures:

### Content: Verbal/Visual

The verbal quality of words consists in their abstract, alphabetic, and symbolic character. The verbal is more cerebral, more linear, and more predictably sequential than the visual. The visual is based on the eye and a sense of place and viewpoint in the objective world.

### Scale: Subordinate/Dominant

Because a word in its pure alphabetic form is a mental construct, its impact is relatively immune to the effect of size. But the emotional immediacy which is the domain of the visual is powerfully affected by size. In this morphology, pictures are assumed to have size-dominance in the normal word/picture relationship.

### Grouping: Regular/Irregular

The basic grouping of words is regular in spacing and alignment, and left-to-right in sequence. There is no basic grouping order for a picture; therefore a picture's organization follows no prescribed order.

### Dimensionality: Flat/Spatial

A word in its basic form gives no illusion of three-dimensional space. It is conceived in a flat plane and depends on a two-dimensional spatial organization in the same plane as the characters themselves. Pictures involving objects inevitably involve also representation in space. It is unnatural, but not impossible, to represent words in an illusionistic manner; it is also not natural, though possible, to bring the representation of objects into a flat plane.

### Message: Informational/Expressive

Words and pictures can each have either a more informational, or objective, message or a more expressive, or emotional, message. In this morphology we are saying that words tend to be normally more informational and pictures more expressive.

This diagram of the word/picture dichotomy dramatizes the classic word/picture contrast. The cool, cerebral, precise, abstract quality of words (below) stands out in contrast to the hot, immediate, visually tangible expressional force of the picture (right).

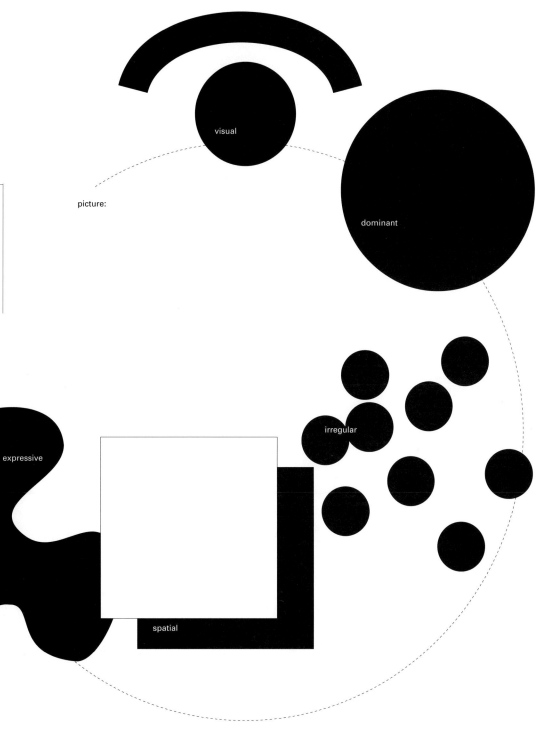

word:

| verbal | **v** |
| --- | --- |
| subordinate | • |
| regular | ⦂⦂⦂ |
| flat | ▢ |
| informational | **i** |

picture:

visual

dominant

expressive

irregular

spatial

*All functioning relationships are a tension between factors of similarity and difference, but for a communication to be clear, it seems that contrast must be the dominant element.*
*—kh*

1

Three examples which
maintain the classic word/
picture contrast.
1.  words as caption
2.  words as label
3.  integrated words

**THE UNBREAKABLE
CUP**

## Analogous/Contrasting Relationships

The three examples above adhere to the classic distinction between words and pictures. Twenty-one examples beginning on page 84 explore this range. They culminate with inversions in which words are pushed to assume primarily visual quality or pictures formulated to have abstract, symbolic qualities of words. Words can dominate and pictures can be subordinate in scale. Words can be erratically patterned and pictures comparatively regimented. It is unnatural, but not impossible, to represent words in an illusionistic manner; it is also not natural, but possible, to bring the representation of objects into a flat plane. Finally, words could be the expressive emotional component against a highly objective, informational picture.

The inversions show that the normal is not absolute, but that establishing a norm puts them in perspective. It then becomes possible to make a more deliberate exploration of relationships that could dramatize a communication even more effectively.

A word/picture relationship can have other qualities as well. Morphologies as they are used in this book are not intended to be exhaustive; each situation will call for adjustments. Thus qualities that define historical difference, for example, or identify a relationship as supportive or subversive, could be added. But the qualities listed here can be considered basic and almost universally applicable. They offer a matrix of simple but powerful relational qualities to keep in mind and to keep the movement of ideas fluid.

In defining the relationship between the elements in a word/

# THE UNBREAKABLE
## cup

THE
UN-
BREAK-
ABLE

**cup**

picture setting, it is useful to define the respects in which they are *analogous*, reflecting or echoing similar qualities, or *contrasting*, possessing primarily different qualities. In reality, and depending on the level of subtlety being observed, a relationship is usually more complex, with qualities of similarity and difference present in both elements to varying degrees.

You will find other relational qualities besides the ones accounted for in the morphological summaries accompanying the examples. In a successful image synthesis, the combination of factors cannot be accounted for by merely cataloging them; it is necessary to keep the morphology in perspective as a tool for either analysis or expansion. Comments have been added to further describe the synthesis of form.

The purpose of every relationship is to convey a message with impact and resulting memorability.

There is more to achieving memorability as an overall image quality than creating a morphologically correct order. It goes beyond analysis to a sense of the whole that comes out of an intuitive grasp and a personal ability to synthesize a statement. An image that asserts a compelling presence will show clear characteristics of formal tension, but characteristics of formal tension are not per se the basis for such a presence. Otherwise, recipes for good images would be possible: they aren't.

Morphologies are only tools for planning or analysis, a kind of coarse thinking to get a sense of alternatives.

In the summary tables accompanying each example, a dotted connecting line indicates a primarily analogous relationship, a slash indicates a primarily contrasting relationship. Where parts of the verbal message change in character, the tables reflect these differences.

| | Words | | | Picture |
|---|---|---|---|---|
| | *The Unbreakable* | | *Cup* | |
| content: | V ·················· V | | / | ☞ |
| scale: | • | / | ● ················· ● | |
| grouping: | ⠿ | / | ⁚⁚ ················· ⁚⁚ | |
| dimensionality: | ☐ | / | ◻ ················· ◻ | |
| message: | ⚘ | / | ⚘ ················· ⚘ | |

contrasting     analogous

|  | Words | | Picture |
| --- | --- | --- | --- |
|  | *The Unbreakable* | *Cup* |  |
| content: | v ···················· v | / | ☏ |
| scale: | · / ● ·················· ● | | ● |
| grouping: | ⠿ ··················· ⠿ | / | ⁙ |
| dimensionality: | ☐ ·················· ☐ | / | ❏ |
| message: | i / ♣ | / | i |

In a simple inversion of the classic distinction, the expressive action centers in the typographic cluster while the photograph in this context is more informational. The arrangement brings the two type clusters, the handle, and the larger broken form—all of which function formally as dots—into a sequential rhythm.

THE
UN  •
BREAK  •
ABLE

cup

|  | Words | | Picture |
|---|---|---|---|
|  | *The Unbreakable* | *Cup* |  |
| content: | v / | ☁·······☁ | |
| scale: | • / | ●·······● | |
| grouping: | ⦂⦂⦂ / | ⁙·······⁙ | |
| dimensionality: | ☐·······☐ / | ☐ | |
| message: | i / | ⚡ / | i |

The composition gets its
strength from the
resonance of arcs, but
more specifically the two
thinner ones at lower right,
a light arc that lifts the cup,
and the one created by the
lower right corner of the
photograph overlapping
the letter *p*.

THE UNBREAKABLE

cup

| | Words | | Picture |
|---|---|---|---|
| | *The Unbreakable* | *Cup* | |
| content: | v ···················· v | / | ☏ |
| scale: | · | / | ● ················· ● |
| grouping: | ⊞ | / | ⁙ ················· ⊞ |
| dimensionality: | ☐ | / | ❑ ················· ❑ |
| message: | i | / | ❧ ················· ❧ |

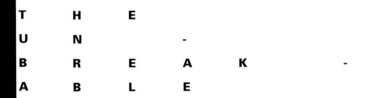

The interweaving of the
word *cup* with the picture
plane produces a play
on dimensionality. The way
all elements are oriented in
relation to the left
boundary heightens their
size and shape contrast.

T    H    E

U    N     -

B   R   E   A   K    -

A   B   L   E

|  | Words | | Picture |
|---|---|---|---|
|  | *The Unbreakable* | *Cup* |  |
| content: | v | / | ☎ ···················· ☎ |
| scale: | · | / | ● | / | · |
| grouping: | ⠿ | / | ⁙ ··················· ⁙ |
| dimensionality: | ☐ ···················· ☐ ··················· ☐ |
| message: | ❧ ···················· ❧ | / | i |

Scale contrast concentrates attention on the photograph; it now has a more distant and informational quality set in a contrasting word environment.

| | Words | | | Picture |
|---|---|---|---|---|
| | *The Unbreakable* | *Cup* | | |
| content: | v ···················· v | | / | 👁 |
| scale: | · | ● ···················· ● | / | ● |
| grouping: | ⠿ ···················· ⠿ | | / | ⁖ |
| dimensionality: | ❑ ···················· ❑ | | ❑ | |
| message: | i ···················· i | | / | ⚘ |

The breaking of the words around the frame relates to the breaking of the cup, but their orderliness contrasts to it.

| | Words | | Picture |
|---|---|---|---|
| | *The Unbreakable* | *Cup* | |
| content: | V ···················· V | / | ☜ |
| scale: | · / | ● ···················· ● | |
| grouping: | ⊞ ···················· ⊞ | / | ⁙ |
| dimensionality: | ❏ ············· ❏ ············· | | ❏ |
| message: | i / | ⚹ ···················· ⚹ | |

Pivoting on a point is the
key picture characteristic
used as a basis to configure
the words.

T  H  E                              B  R  E  A  K  A  B  L  E

          U  N    ·

Cup

| | Words | | | Picture |
| --- | --- | --- | --- | --- |
| | *The Unbreakable* | *Cup* | | |
| content: | v ···················· v | | / | ☏ |
| scale: | • ···················· • | | / | ● |
| grouping: | ⊞ / | ❊· ···················· ⊞ | | |
| dimensionality: | ☐···················· ☐ | | / | ❑ |
| message: | i / | ❖ ···················· ❖ | | |

The irregular cup contour
in relation to its straight
top is the key to the type
arrangement.

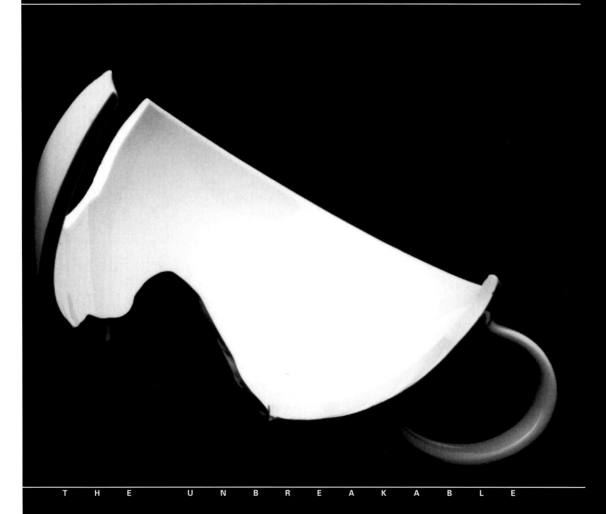

T  H  E     U  N  B  R  E  A  K  A  B  L  E

c      Uᵖ

| | Words | | | Picture |
|---|---|---|---|---|
| | *The Unbreakable* | *Cup* | | |
| content: | v ···················· v | | / | ☁ |
| scale: | · | / | ● ················· | ● |
| grouping: | �֍ ·················· ✖ | | ·················· | ✖ |
| dimensionality: | ▱ | / | ▢ | / | ▱ |
| message: | ⚡ ·················· ⚡ | | ·················· | ⚡ |

The implosive colliding of
two cup fragments is
contrasted to the scattering
of the type elements.

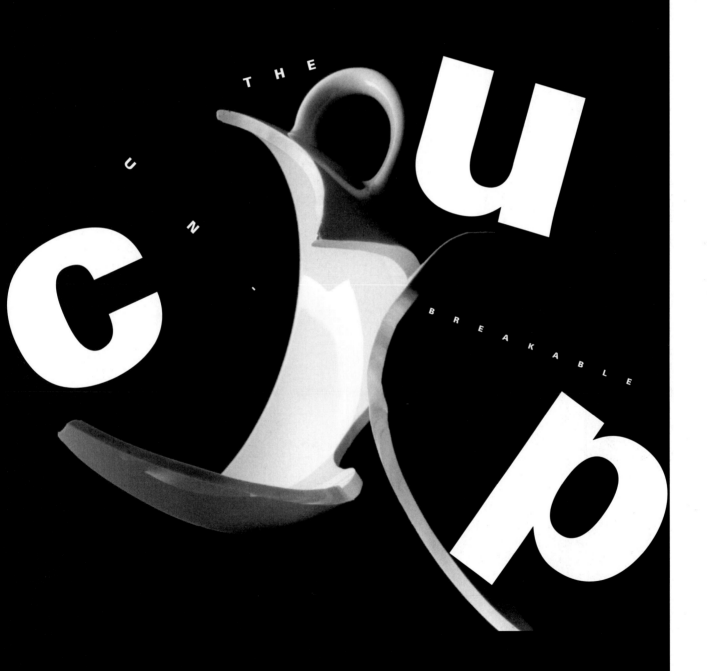

| | Words | | | Picture |
|---|---|---|---|---|
| | *The Unbreakable* | *Cup* | | |
| content: | v ···················· v | | / | ☁ |

| | Words | | | Picture |
|---|---|---|---|---|
| | *The Unbreakable* | *Cup* | | |
| content: | v ················· v | | / | ☎ |
| scale: | • ················· • | | / | ● |
| grouping: | ⁂ ················· ⁂ ················· | | | ⁂ |
| dimensionality: | ☐ ·············· ☐ | | / | ◳ |
| message: | i ················· i | | / | ♣ |

The words pick up an
alignment from the cup. As
dots they refer to the
texture of the rock. In its
receding scale, the type
goes toward extinction, the
ultimate breakup.

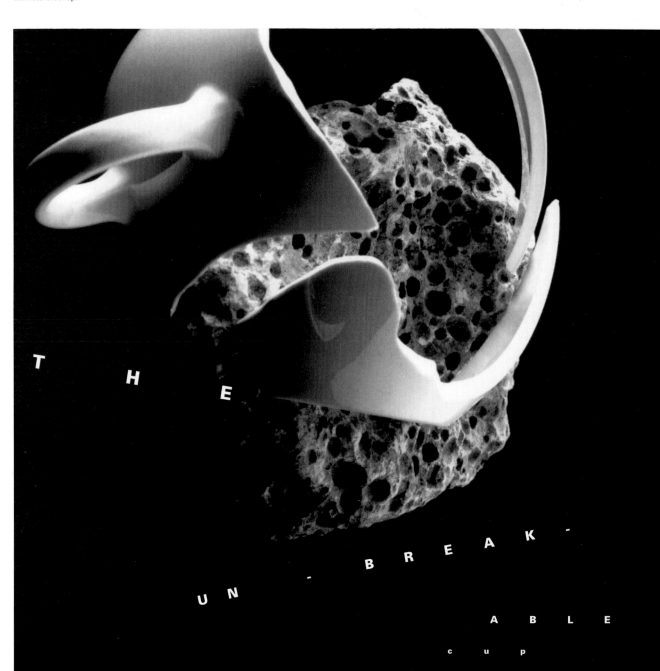

T    H                    E

                              U N      -    B R E A K  -

                                              A    B L    E

                                         c    u    p

|  | **Words** | | | | **Picture** |
|---|---|---|---|---|---|
|  | *The* | *Unbreakable* | *Cup* | | |
| content: | v ·········· v ·········· v | | | / | ☜ |
| scale: | • ·········· • ·········· • | | | / | ● |
| grouping: | ▦ / ⁘ / ▦ | | | / | ⁘ |
| dimensionality: | ☐ / ❏ / ☐ | | | / | ❏ |
| message: | i / ✿ / i | | | / | ✿ |

*The cup* as a definition;
*unbreakable* as a mocking,
mimicking line.

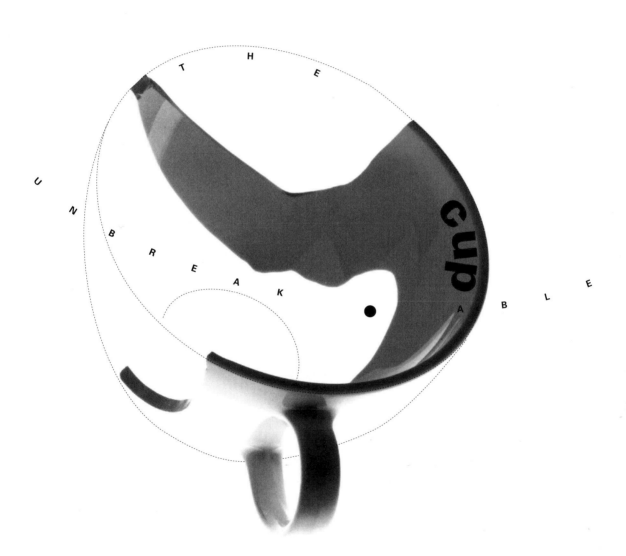

|  | Words | | Picture |
|---|---|---|---|
|  | *The Unbreakable* | *Cup* |  |
| content: | 👁 ·········· 👁 | 👁 |
| scale: | · / ● ·········· ● |  |
| grouping: | ⁘ ·········· ⁘ ·········· ⁙ |  |
| dimensionality: | ▢ / ◪ ·········· ◪ |  |
| message: | ⚘ ·········· ⚘ ·········· ⚘ |  |

The cup in its broken state
becomes a vessel to
contain broken type.

| | Words: | | Picture |
| --- | --- | --- | --- |
| | *The Unbreakable* | *Cup* | |
| content: | v | / ☊·········· | ☊ |
| scale: | · ·········· ● | ·········· ● | |
| grouping: | ⁘ / | ⁝⁝⁝ / | ⁘ |
| dimensionality: | ❑ / | ☐ / | ❑ |
| message: | ✂ / | i / | ✂ |

The prefix *un* reads bi-directionally: to the small type because of its black kinship, despite the large distance; to *cup* where it defines it as an *uncup*. The bar, borrowed from the grid of the background, is, by its color and flatness, part of the typographic language. The type elements give the sensation of falling while the cup itself is essentially static.

THE
BREAKABLE

cup
i
UN

| | Words | | Picture | |
|---|---|---|---|---|
| | *The Unbreakable* | | *Cup* | |
| content: | v | / | ☂ ···················· ☂ | |
| scale: | • ························· ● | | ● ···················· ● | |
| grouping: | ⁞⁞⁞ | / | ⁖ ···················· ⁖ | |
| dimensionality: | ☐ | / | ◲ ···················· ◲ | |
| message: | i | / | ⚘ ···················· ⚘ | |

A period defines a
declarative statement; the
repeat of the periods
reiterates the declaration—
but visually it breaks up and
relates to the digitization of
the picture. The large *C* is a
surrogate whole cup; the
solarized image is a decrepit
shadow.

T H E
U.N.B.R.E.A.K.A.B.L.E

| | Words | | | Picture |
| --- | --- | --- | --- | --- |
| | *The Unbreakable* | *Cup* | | |
| content: | v ···················· v | | / | ☂ |
| scale: | ● ···················· ● ···················· ● |
| grouping: | ⁙ ···················· ⁙ ···················· ⁙ |
| dimensionality: | ❑ ···················· ❑ ···················· ❑ |
| message: | ⚘ ···················· ⚘ ···················· ⚘ |

Part of the text is shifted to
the picture plane, where it is
broken by the cup fragment—
which by comparison is
paradoxically complete. A
brightness zone, where the
picture plane meets the word
*cup*, stresses the brittle
vulnerability of the cup and
unifies the composite image.

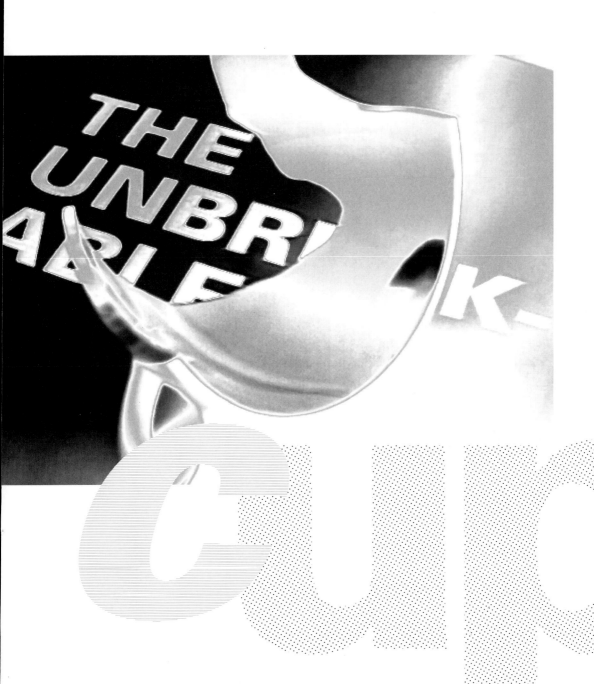

| The | Un- | breakable | Cup |
| --- | --- | --- | --- |
| v / | ☜ ☜ | ☜ | ☜ |
| • • | • / | ● | ● |
| ⊞ / | ✾ ✾ | ✾ | ✾ |
| ☐ | ☐ ☐ | ☐ | ☐ |
| i / | ⚘ ⚘ | ⚘ | ⚘ |

Except for the article, all elements are lost in the visual—where sequence matters less and the dotlike letters and dotted large letters merge into the matrix of the picture's dots. The clarity of *the* is required to alert to the fact that there is other information to decipher. The ominous quality stems in large part from the picture image being upside down. (Invert the book to see the original orientation.)

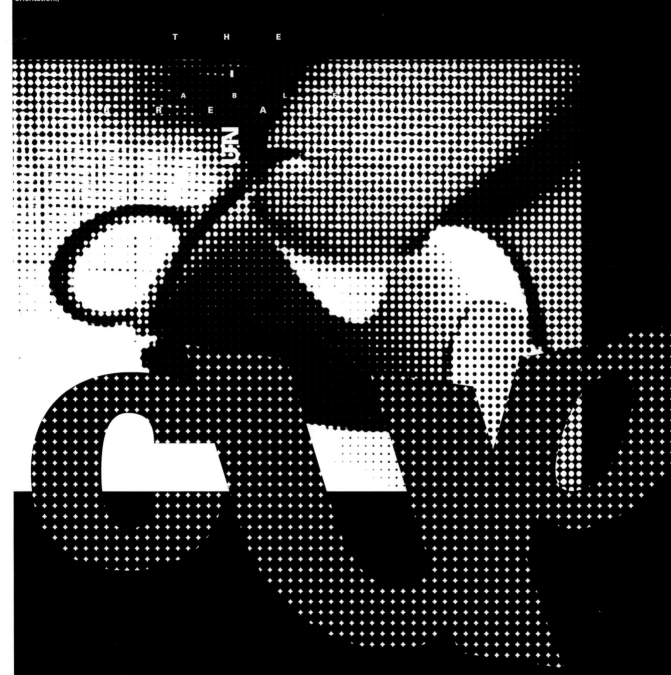

T H E

| | Words | | | | Picture |
|---|---|---|---|---|---|
| | *The Unbreakable* | | *Cup* | | |
| content: | 👁 | / | v | / | 👁 |
| scale: | · | / | ● | ·········· | ● |
| grouping: | ✻ | ·········· | ✻ | ·········· | ✻ |
| dimensionality: | ▢ | ·········· | ▢ | ·········· | ▢ |
| message: | ✿ | ·········· | ✿ | ·········· | ✿ |

The randomized
letterforms express
breaking. The hairline rules
speed up the motion.

T    H    E

U N    B    R

E A  K    A

B L E

| | Words | | Picture |
|---|---|---|---|
| | *The Unbreakable* | *Cup* | |
| content: | ☂ ........... | ☂ ........... | ☂ |
| scale: | ● ........... | ● ........... | ● |
| grouping: | ⁂ ........... | ⁂ ........... | ⁂ |
| dimensionality: | ☐ ........... | ☐ ........... | ☐ |
| message: | ♣ ........... | ♣ ........... | ♣ |

The words merge with the
textural grain of the image.

| | Words | | | Picture |
| --- | --- | --- | --- | --- |
| | *The Unbreakable* | *Cup* | | |
| content: | V ···················· V | | / | ☜ |
| scale: | · | / | ● ···················· ● | |
| grouping: | ⠿ | / | ⁂ ···················· ⁂ | |
| dimensionality: | ☐ | / | ❏ ···················· ❏ | |
| message: | ✿ ···················· ✿ ···················· ✿ | | | |

Both the picture segment and the word segment are each in their way self-quoting: the picture by bringing the object into a picture environment where it is presented as a flat image; the words by embedding the modifying text into the noun. The strong diagonal striping is an obvious link, but the bridging near the small type is important for the synthesis.

| Words | | | | Picture |
|---|---|---|---|---|
| *The* | *Un-* | *breakable* | *Cup* | |

The feather as a soft counter-element is alluded to in the type structure— it is light and is oriented along a central shaft. The negative forms of the word *cup* relate to the feather rhythm on a cruder scale and stabilize the composition.

The explosive moment of a concussion brings all elements—including the morphology table—into a single expressive, radiating image.

The chaos of falling
extends to every element.
The underlying *c* form is a
stabilizing point of
orientation.

# 4.

*Texture and pattern are universally attractive aspects of visual form.*

*A study trip to the Oaxaca Valley (Wah-Ha'-Kah) of Mexico provides the context for this project. Using a daily sketch routine and a combination of intentional and chance methods, impressions and place/time data are overlaid. Textures and patterns are derived from drawings, rubbings, and photographs.*

*After returning home, the sketchbook images are processed into a more definite form. These forms stimulate probes\* into fresh combinations, suggesting new potential for graphic expression.*

---

\*probe:
> investigate, delve, dig, examine, feel out, grope, hunt, inquire, look, observe, peer, pursue, research, scan, scrutinize, search, seek, sound, study, test.

All examples are by the author.

**• Technical Notes:**
The notations were drawn as described on page 111 and scanned as 8-bit scans for placement in PageMaker®. The patterns on pages 117–19 and the dissolves of these throughout this chapter were drawn in Canvas®. Scans of photographs made with Hyperscan® were combined with the patterns in Hypercard® to produce the images on pages 121–23, 127, 130–31, 135–36. Photographs were the source of some scans; objects scanned using an 8mm video camera and MacVision® were also combined. Applescan® was used to customize screens on pages 126 and 128. Some pages were composed in FreeHand®, others directly in the final layout program, PageMaker®.

Texture is the characteristic repetitive physical structure given to a material by the size, shape, arrangement, and proportions of its granular parts. Grain can be considered its microcosmic level, texture the overall effect of the grain, and pattern the macrolevel, at which grain and texture are used to complete a larger repetition.

It is the texture of a city that makes it human, the texture of food that makes it appetizing. But a gritty texture may not be far from a crunchy one; one may be appealing, the other repellent, or appealing to one person and repellent to another.

Texture is meaningless apart from its context. A smooth path through the woods, rough cobblestone in the city, nuts in a smooth ice cream sundae—the contrast creates the appeal.

One of the joys of visiting other cultures in sunny climates is seeing such things as the slatted shelters breaking up shadows into bits or stripes, transforming objects struck by the off-and-on of light.

Texture is not virtuosic; there isn't a single player. It's the masses, the people, the many. There is something democratic and accessible about it, resisting categorization. There is an immediate familiarity, a welcoming.

Texture enlists the scanning action of the eyes—reading, searching, delighting in the tangibility of the surface. It is the texture of text that makes reading a pleasure—if it is rightly organized for reading, for communicating.

## . . . and Some Questions

Because people react spontaneously to textured surface, the temptation to overuse, or use only to beguile, by fakery and excess, is enormous. When is texture an agent of deceit and when a legitimate communicative feature? Does texture add meaningfully to complexity? When is texture a misdirected or excessive complexity, concealing more than revealing, veiling more than opening? What is a good relationship of concealing and revealing?

If texture gives easy access, is a response to texture likely to be a superficial one? Is it a failure to see globally? Is it wrong for a texture to become immediately obvious?

There are connotations concerning texture that make its use suspect: is it materialistic, merely pretty, covering a structural defect?

Does texture elicit a more emotional response, and pattern a more intellectual one, or are both by their decorative tendencies on the emotional side?

---

## Project 4 Summary:

### Personal Goals:

**To use a travel experience as means of renewal and extension of design vocabulary.**

**To create a useful program of registering visual impressions, referred to as notations.**

**To allow for chance factors to affect choices.**

**To experiment freely with new visual material.**

Process: See pages 111 and 120.

**On the 70th birthday of Hostess cupcakes, curlicue creator D. R. Rice, age 83, finally explained why he chose it: "A straight stripe didn't look rich enough, so we tried the squiggle."**

**—Reported in the Philadelphia Inquirer**

Is it visually better or merely different for houses of the Costa del Sol or the Greek Islands to be painted over with white— concealing, or at least reducing the perception of, the texture of the stucco or plaster? Teotihuacan and Monte Albán—the Mexican temple sites— were not originally as we see them today. They were stuccoed over and smooth and painted. Does the reduction of texture equal greater cultural refinement? Or is the opposite true? Or neither?

Is there a correlation between texture and intimacy? Texture is used to "warm" an object or an image. Is this an inherent quality? Does texture open up a field and give the eye more room, more places to go? What does the congestion of popular mass communications tell us about human interest in and/or tolerance for congested texture? Does being lost in a lot of activity give comfort or does it estrange? Does the reading of texture postpone or hasten the reading of a page? Serif types are more complex, more textural; yet they do not impede legibility. In fact, rightly applied, these features promote legibility.

Whether a texture is good, clear, effective, appropriate depends on judgments informed by considering these questions.

Finally, it's what "works," and every process should be open enough so we can find what "works."

## Grain, Texture, Pattern

At what distance does grain become texture, and texture become pattern? When does the expression of the grain become gestural, drawing too much attention to itself? When is it suppressed into being mere background, insignificant to the whole?

And what incidence of repetition is decisive for separating repetitive from individual form? The "magic number" $\pm 7$ is referred to as the dividing line between the few and the many. The actual number depends on the nature and configuration of the units. Interesting patterns are the product of a flux between perception as individual units and a larger composite.

We can refer to the overall texture of an image just as we refer to its color. Usually we mean the finesse of the range of form used. But texture at the microlevel is not gestural, except as its boundaries are determined by shape. Without shape, it bears little analogy to the human gesture, to the body—the analogy required for a significant accord with universal human experience.

Design requires the clear integration of texture in relation to larger pattern, shape, and the overall image.

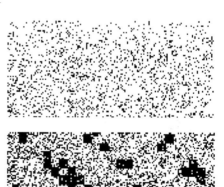

In the progression from grain to texture to pattern, individual elements gain identity.

**Grain and Repro Processes.** The reproduction of images requires that they be broken into smaller discrete parts, the fineness dependent on the reproduction mechanism. All commercial invention strives for units so small the eye will not perceive them, so that no "instrument" for the conveyance of the image will be felt. But artistic invention strives for an authentic interaction between instrument and expression. The degree of resolution appropriate for an expression is not simply or necessarily the finest possible by the affordable technology; the appropriate resolution is the one in which the grain of the image agrees with what it is supposed to express.

Just as over-refinement of food or manners can become physically or psychologically unhealthy, the smoothness of image can be too sweet, too slick, too ideal, and inhuman. Or it gets too precious and untouchable. Of course, there is a place for high resolution—this is not an argument against it. But there is also a need to counteract high resolution as an end in itself. So it is a special concern of the graphic artist to make judgments about the rightness of the grain in relation to image rather than—as the commercial tendency is—to see constantly finer grain as an inherently superior trend. Bold new moves in architecture and design often come from reverting to simpler, more basic, design.

The grain may be inherent in the content of an image, such as a weaving or a field of grasses, but there is also the grain of the image-carrier itself, where a friction is established between it and naturalistic representation. The processing of this friction, of understanding how it alludes in its own way to the object or contradicts it, is important. Reconciling this discrepancy/correlation conflict is part of the excitement and the basis for memorable communication.

**Music and Texture.** What is the relation of texture to timbre in music? Are there visual equivalents to reedy sounds— oboe, saxophone, clarinet—or to brass sounds like the tuba, trumpet, or horn; or to strings, timpani, or celesta? If finding clear equivalents is impossible, can qualities nevertheless be described by similar adjectives and evaluated by similar criteria? Can the morphology of visual texture described here also be applied to music and verbal language?

Regarding the universal artistic problem of adjusting texture to larger pattern and structure, the cellist Yo-Yo Ma describes how, in listening to great singers, he could sense the way solo voices could penetrate or float above the mass of orchestra sound. He was able to succeed in creating an extraordinary relationship between his instrument, the solo cello, and the symphony orchestra by building from these observations and analytically pursuing the effect of speed and weight of his bowing on the vibrato, changing components by small amounts. The true musician, he observes, has to think big and small at the same time. As performer he accounts for the single events, but he can't neglect identifying with the composer who accounts for the balancing of the whole.

Of course, it is this subjugation of detail to the whole that allows us to perceive it as music rather than just an instrument.

" . . . everything in the (semantic and lyric) structure is respected; and yet nothing seduces, nothing persuades us to enjoyment; this is an excessively expressive art . . . and thereby it never transcends culture; . . . for the body to accompany the musical diction . . . by a 'gesture-notice'— that is what is difficult, especially since all of musical pedagogy teaches not the 'grain' of the voice but the emotive modes of its emission: this is the myth of breath.

" . . . it is in the throat, site where the phonic metal hardens and assumes its contour, it is in the facial mask that *signifying* breaks out, producing not the soul but enjoyment. In Fischer-Dieskau's performance, I seem to hear only the lungs, never the tongue, the glottis, the teeth, the sinuses, the nose."
—Roland Barthes, "The Grain of the Voice"

"I don't think about texture; it just happens while I try to reconcile layers of a painting."
—Warren Rohrer, in conversation about his "field of color" paintings.

Six basic aspects of
texture expressed as
pairs of opposites.
The primary words
such as *coarse : fine*
refer more to visual
syntax; visual qualities
are stressed. The
secondary words, in
parantheses, refer
more to their semantic
quality; meaning is
stressed.

What are the expressions of grain, texture, and pattern in
a two-dimensional surface? Six pairs of contrasts can help
to clarify one's intentions, as well as to assist in reading
what is actually happening in a textural image. By
comparing these syntactic or formal features with their
semantic or expressive aspects, we can better sense
their potential for meaning as compared to decoration.

For instance, it is one thing to make an arbitrary decision for
an amorphous or geometric grain, texture, or pattern—on
the basis of preference—but it is quite different to
associate the choice of geometric with the *intention* of
showing something constructed as compared to something
natural.

In contrasting grains, textures, or patterns in terms of their
naturalness or geometricity, it will also be important to
create the right degree of fineness or scatteredness to create
effective relationship. It is therefore a combination of
qualities which work for clarity; the features listed in the
morphology can be combined in any way.

In the examples on this page, the comparison of how a change
in attributes affects the visual image is clear because the
comparison is tightly controlled. In the examples beginning page 121, more complex interactions are shown. In
those cases the operative attributes are less clear and more
subject to interpretation. This does not diminish the value
of naming the attributes as a way to decide how changes in
an image can be made.

Using texture consists in making value judgments. By
naming the qualities it is possible to explore changes
intelligently: for example, "make it looser," "make it more
geometric," "make it finer."

| | | | : | |
|---|---|---|---|---|
| unit size | *(raw)* **coarse** | : | **fine** *(refined)* |
| proximity | *(scattered)* **loose** | : | **tight** *(concentrated)* |
| arrangement | *(accidental)* **random** | : | **patterned** *(intentional)* |
| unit shape | *(natural)* **amorphous** | : | **geometric** *(constructed)* |
| content | *(symbolic)* **abstract** | : | **representational** *(iconic)* |
| physicality | *(immediate)* **flat** | : | **illusionary** *(simulated)* |

An image can be
characterized as having
qualities primarily
on one side of a pair, or
of having a tension of
contrast involving both
sides of a pair.

This image of small
dots (units) is generally
fine, loose, amorphous,
abstract and flat,
but there is a tension
between its being
random in the arrange-
ment of the secondary
unit and repetitious in
the pattern.

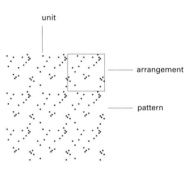

| | | | |
|---|---|---|---|
| unit size | | | fine |
| proximity | | loose : | tight |
| arrangement | | random : | patterned |
| unit shape | | | geometric |
| content | | abstract | |
| physicality | | flat | |

The attributes of this
texture are identical to
the one above except
for the removal of the
*random : patterned*
contrast. Patterning
dominates.

| | | | |
|---|---|---|---|
| unit size | | | fine |
| proximity | | loose : | tight |
| arrangement | | | patterned |
| elements | | | geometric |
| content | | abstract | |
| physicality | | flat | |

I travel to be surprised, amazed. The surprise and amazement has to get back into my work: agitate it (me); refresh it (me); change it (me) unexpectedly.

How will I confront the temptation to just take it all in without processing it? Or to bring my preconception to the new place?

How will I be able to feel good about the trip five years from now? How can I draw inspiration to which I can constantly refer? What does it mean to bring something back—other than snapshots and souvenirs? Can I program an activity of registering impressions using previous experience with visual notations, yet be truly receptive to the new experience?

This project shows one way of establishing a pattern for travel notations and subsequent processing of the material discovered on one day. While each day yields a different set of images, I have found the concerns to be unconsciously overlapping. Several concerns emerge as especially important to me. In this case, in Mexico, texture was one. I have not used texture extensively myself, and I have envied people who use it well. I envy craftsmen whose processes yield accidental textural qualities in addition to the intentional ones. This project is thus a demonstration of an approach to widening a personal horizon.

**The Virtue of Drawing.** My medium is photography but my memory medium is drawing. I photograph extensively, but drawing affects me differently. The memory of a place I draw is more indelibly etched in my mind. Rather than just registering the effect as in a photograph, actually figuring out how things relate proportionally and spatially is a challenge that makes the mind incredibly active. And for all the instantaneous gratification of photography, no satisfaction is more immediate than an evolving drawing. A drawing seems somehow both more tentative and open. "Drawing means leaving out" is one artist's definition.

**Why Mexico?** Mexico is appealing for several reasons. The complex overlay of cultures and historic epochs has given Mexican culture a complex and enigmatic quality. The proximity of so contrasting a neighbor is intriguing. The country that made the graphic, public mural a major voice of revolution intrigues me. It's a country that so typifies the vast social problems of the late twentieth century. A country of astounding juxtapositions of terrain and culture presents vivid visual contrasts. The pre-Cortés artifacts and sites spring from universal expression.

**Ruins.** Ruins of human artifacts are vaster than both nature and the man-made. They partake of nature but bear the vestiges of man expressing both the enduring aspiration and the durational reality of human experience.

The combination of man-made structure and natural forces is more to me than either alone; it refers not to time past but time that is still in flux, linking the temporal and the infinite. Time renders matter poignantly present by eroding the adamantly willful in the man-made. What most appeals to me of nature is that which shows an intelligence, a logic, a process of human analog at work. Nature marries far more factors in her processes than we can ever envision, much less control. In forecasts of the post-human evolution of animals on earth, our hybrid, domestic ones will soon vanish because the complexity of adaptive features will have been forfeited. As Thoreau put it, "in wildness is the preservation of the world."

Ruins, in their disintegrating state—weathered, eroded, incomplete—show a strong textural quality, a marriage of human structuring and natural counterstructuring. In their incompletenesss they are intensely real and exciting to the imagination at the same time.

Temple ruins are archeological digs of the human mind, expressions of its need for symbols and mythology.

This trip was made during the dry season, when the earth tones, especially ochers and browns, predominate. The dryness gives the whole earth a crumbliness, a rough textural feel.

**Notation Process**  ▶

This procedure is worked out by trial and error at the first site, but the tools are chosen in advance.

Tools:
Sketch pad, 6½ x 10 inches
Pencils of varying color
Fine line marker
French-curve template
Magnetic compass

*A program for daily notations, Mexico, March 9–20, 1989*

*At a site where I am prompted to draw I find a comfortable position, stable for a half-hour, to make a notation. Marks are added to the page in the following sequence.*

*1*
*The time of day is noted in the appropriate vertical grid block row. The hours are numbered 1–24; 10:00 a.m. is therefore the 10th row.*
*2*
*A green dot marks the center of the page. It may later change character or size in relation to the other content.*
*3*
*A perspective drawing is made.*
*4*
*The directional line pointing north is drawn.*
*5*
*Curves selected from the french-curve template are added in three colors: black, green, purple. The image of these curves suggests some other feature of the site and overlays the drawing.*
*6*
*A rubbing of a texture or form found at the site is loosely plotted into the drawing, the actual area of the rubbing evolving as the rubbing progresses.*
*7*
*Place and date are entered in the gridded heading.*

*The chance factors are:*
*—the location of north and hence the determination of the position of the template*
*— the character of the rubbing in relation to the drawing*
*— the secondary images formed by the overlays*
*— the blobs left by the pen*
*— the configuration of the place/date information*

*If each facet of the notation were pushed to greater objectivity and usefulness for communication, what form could it take? In the notation detail on pages 112–16 the evolution from notation component to more defined form for communication is shown.*

1. heading matrix ------ becomes ------ variable grid element
2. place/date ----------- becomes ------ typeface
3. drawing -------------- becomes ------ photo (and vice versa)
4. template ------------- becomes ------ logo
5. rubbing -------------- becomes ------ pattern

The notebook has a grid at the top of each page. It is accepted as one of the elements of the notation.

Blocking in a row to correspond with the time of day introduces another graphic feature.

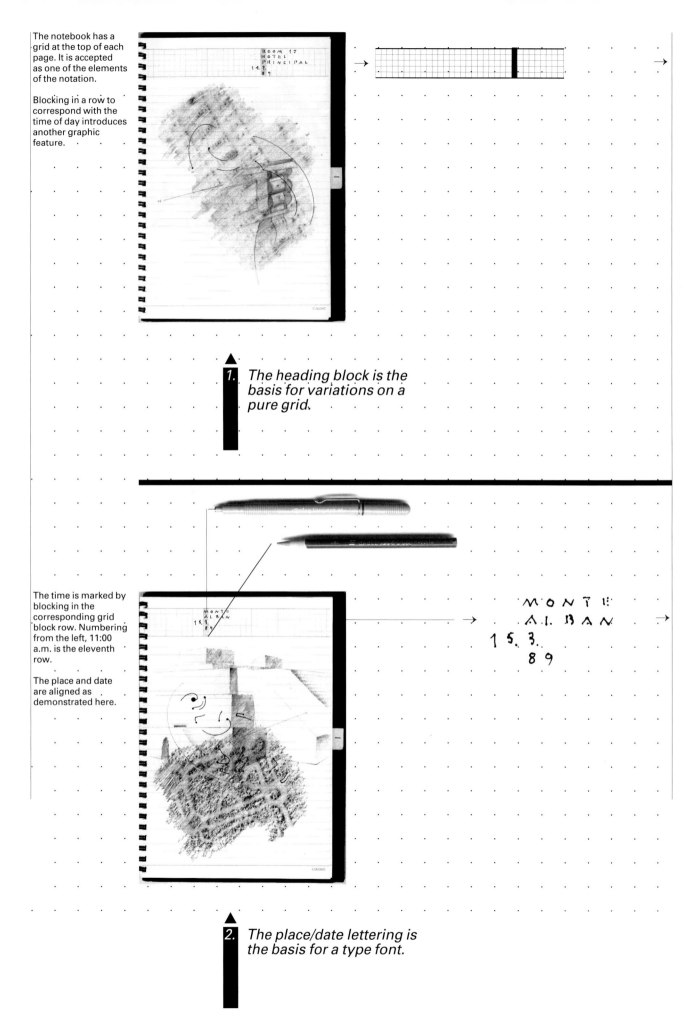

**1.** *The heading block is the basis for variations on a pure grid.*

The time is marked by blocking in the corresponding grid block row. Numbering from the left, 11:00 a.m. is the eleventh row.

The place and date are aligned as demonstrated here.

**2.** *The place/date lettering is the basis for a type font.*

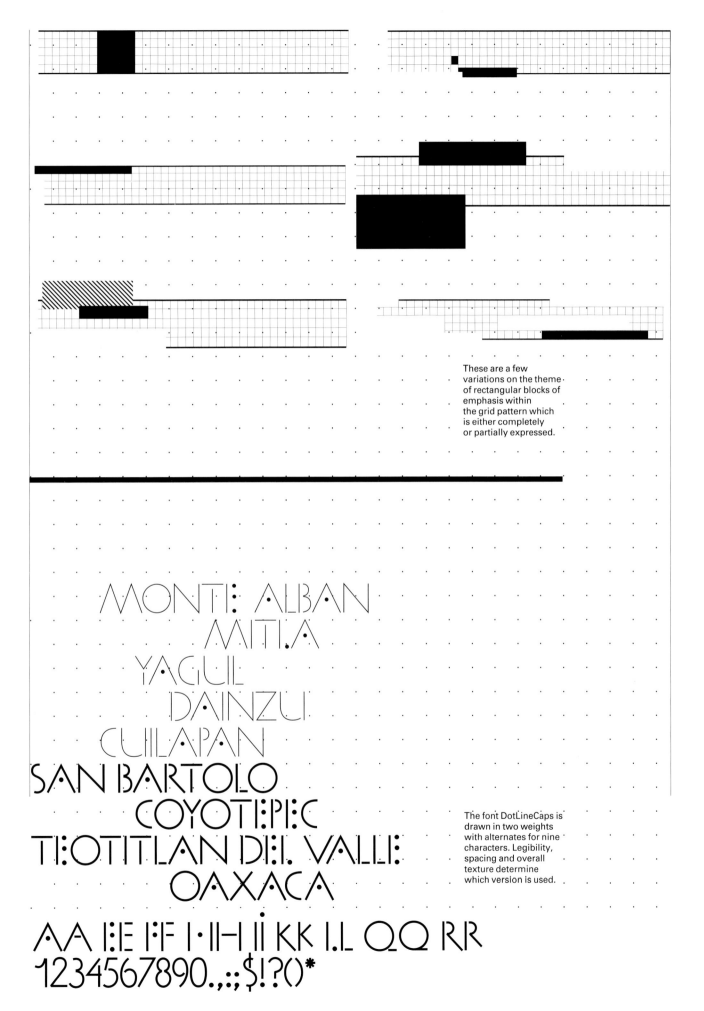

These are a few
variations on the theme
of rectangular blocks of
emphasis within
the grid pattern which
is either completely
or partially expressed.

MONTE ALBAN
MITLA
YAGUL
DAINZU
CUILAPAN
SAN BARTOLO
COYOTEPEC
TEOTITLAN DEL VALLE
OAXACA

The font DotLineCaps is
drawn in two weights
with alternates for nine
characters. Legibility,
spacing and overall
texture determine
which version is used.

AA EE FF I IH II KK LL QQ RR
1234567890.,:;$!?()*

A drawing from observation, with sensitivity to perspective and tonal values, while preserving the linear quality of the pencil, is a preparation for photography. Photography, in turn, is subject to manipulaton that brings it back to the realm of drawing.

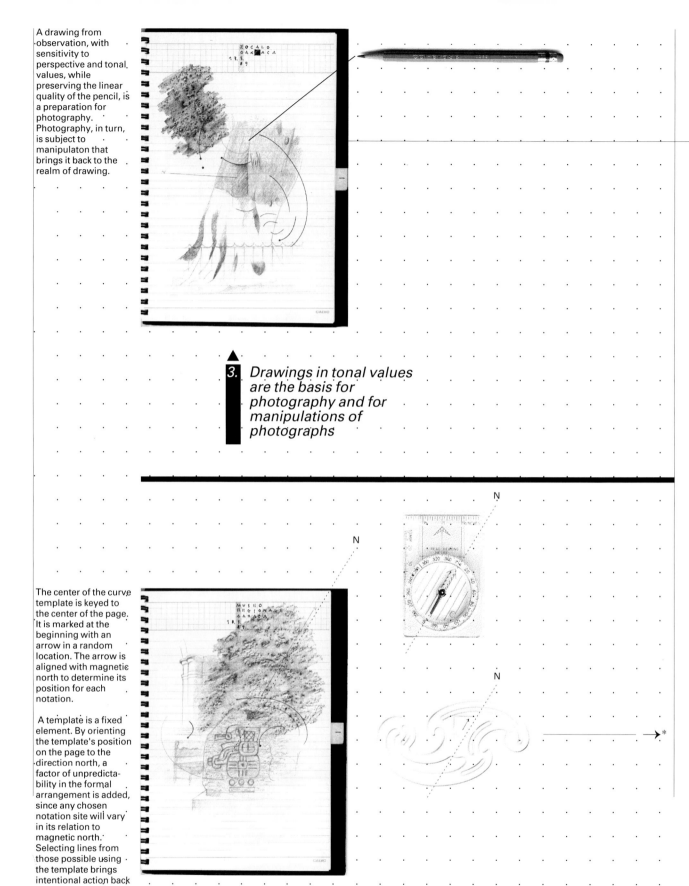

**3.** *Drawings in tonal values are the basis for photography and for manipulations of photographs*

The center of the curve template is keyed to the center of the page. It is marked at the beginning with an arrow in a random location. The arrow is aligned with magnetic north to determine its position for each notation.

A template is a fixed element. By orienting the template's position on the page to the direction north, a factor of unpredictability in the formal arrangement is added, since any chosen notation site will vary in its relation to magnetic north. Selecting lines from those possible using the template brings intentional action back into the notation.

**4.** *A template, as a constant formal element, has qualities of a logotype.*

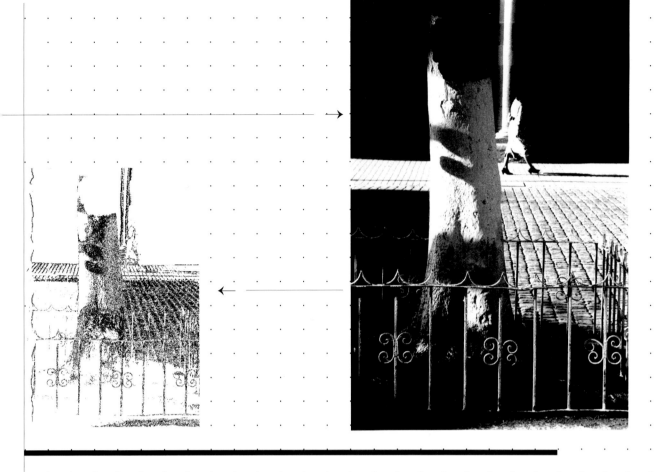

Texture and tonality are applied to the logotype for greater distinction of the letters, resulting in greater textural diversity.

*New content—the word* Mexico— *and the influence of a Zapotec relief sculpture takes it in a new direction.*

*

In the sense of being a stable, constant element, a logo is like a template. Since there was no attempt in the original template choice to create a readable logotype, the connection between the template and what has been adopted here as a logo *is not a direct one.* The idea of an overlay of geometric elements is suggested by the stone relief in the drawing.

A textured surface in the vicinity of the drawing site is the source for a small scale rubbing made with a soft lead pencil. This rubbing was made from a basket with a "Mitla" theme.

I spent my time in Mitla doing photography. Two notations representing Mitla were done in retrospect using the photographs as source. The dual date record refers to the date of the photograph and the later drawing.

The drawing program set up at the beginning of the notation process ensures a continuity with previously done notations.

**5.** *Rubbings, as well as drawings, are sources for patterns created in a computer drawing program.*

*The criterion for these new patterns is not simply the number of permutations possible, but rather those which have a feel traceable to the Mitla sources.*

*All patterns shown are based on a 64-unit module. They are enlarged 400% to bring out a pattern quality, as opposed to the granular quality at the original bit-mapped scale.*

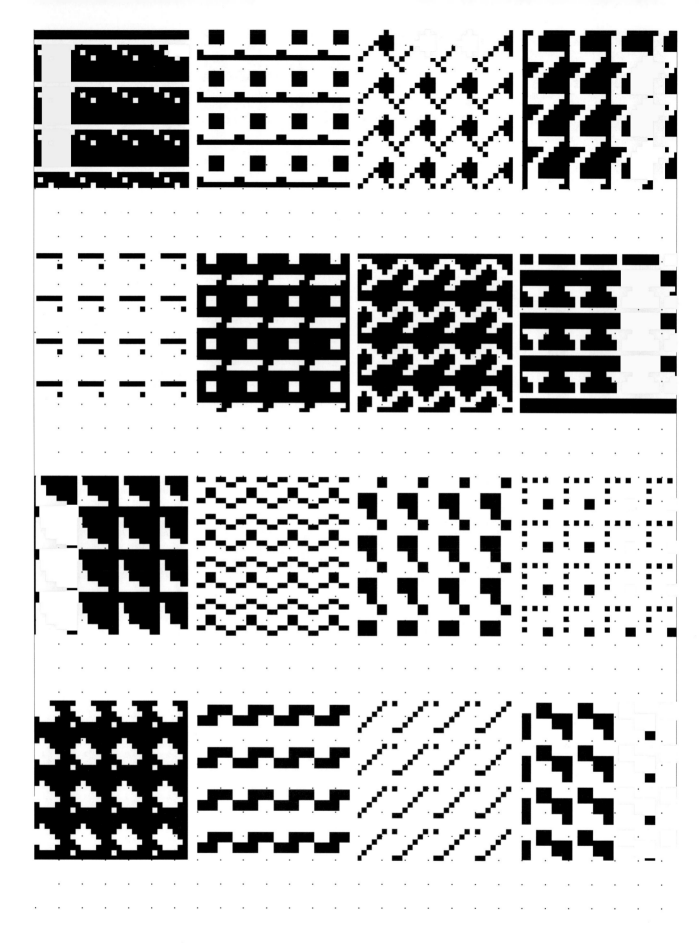

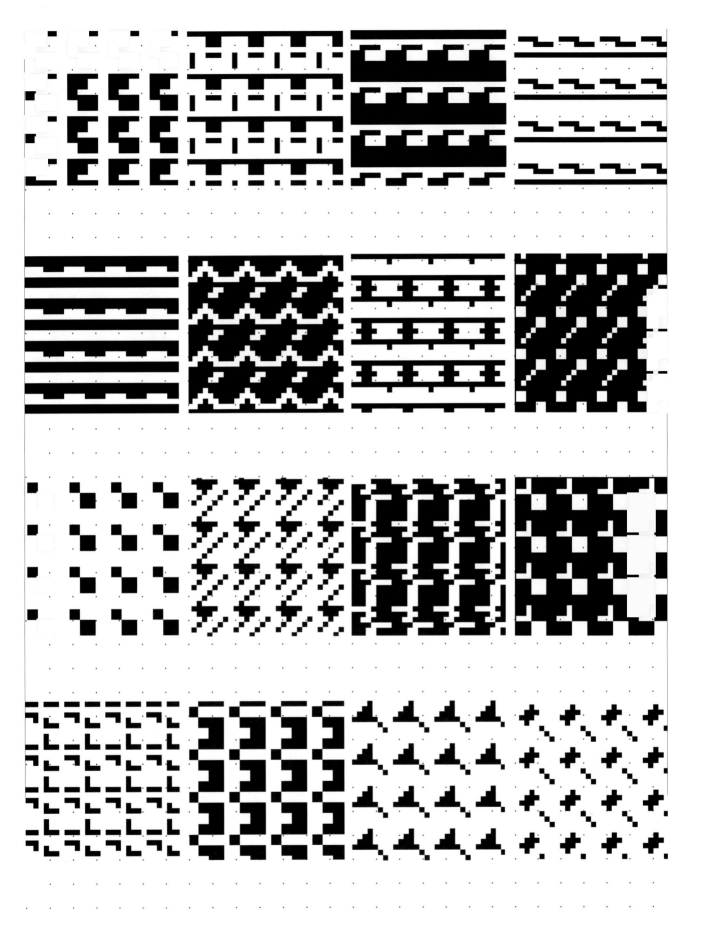

Arranged in order from fine to coarse:

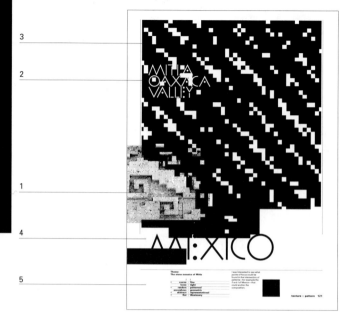

1
A complex mix of textures is created by a halftone screen whose basic increment is a Mitla motif. This is applied to a continuous tone photograph of the actual stone patterns. Though we would normally consider this to be a coarse screen, in this context it is the finest component. The image is representational and shows illusory depth.

2
The type is patterned in one sense—the strokes and dots of the words obey the rhythm of the words. Seen abstractly, however, the structure is relatively random.

3
Within a pattern of diagonal lines, elements are randomly distributed.

4
The scale of type is increased, changing it from a more textural character to a more individual, patterned quality.

5
This single square is the culmination of a progression toward individual forms, departing from pattern.

Proportion and contrast are the key criteria for how one texture relates to another. (A texture can be coarse relative to one texture and fine relative to another, loose in relation to one and tight in relation to another, and so on.)

• Key contrast qualities are marked with a dot in the tables.

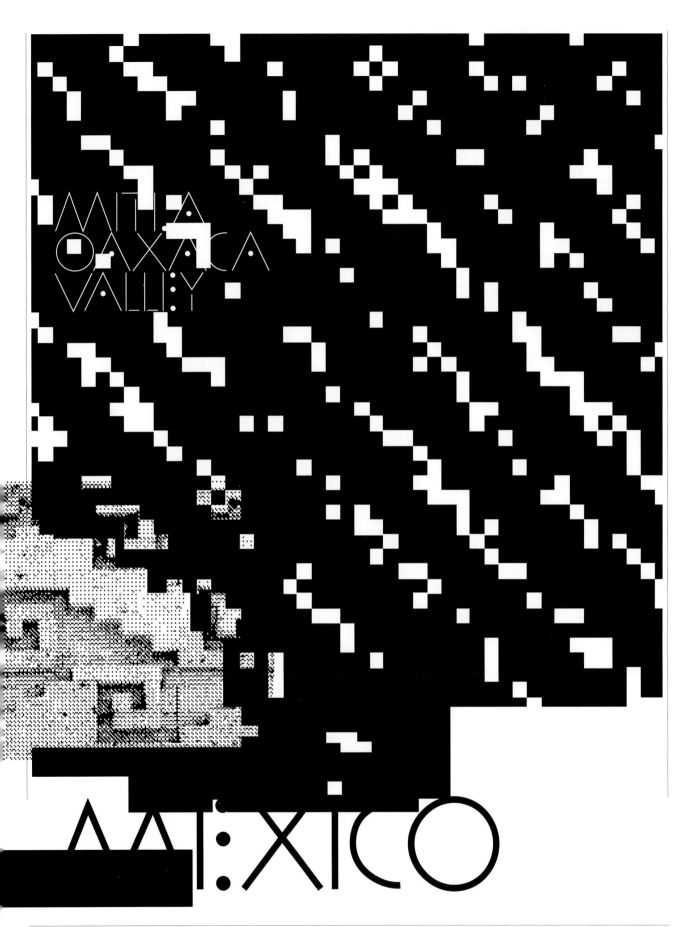

**Theme:**
**The stone mosaics of Mitla**

|   |   |
|---|---|
| • coarse : | **fine** |
| loose : | **tight** |
| • random : | **patterned** |
| amorphous : | **geometric** |
| • abstract : | **representational** |
| • flat : | **illusionary** |

I was interested to see what points of focus could be found in the intersection of patterns—for example the *E* and *I* of Mexico—that could anchor the composition.

**texture :: pattern   121**

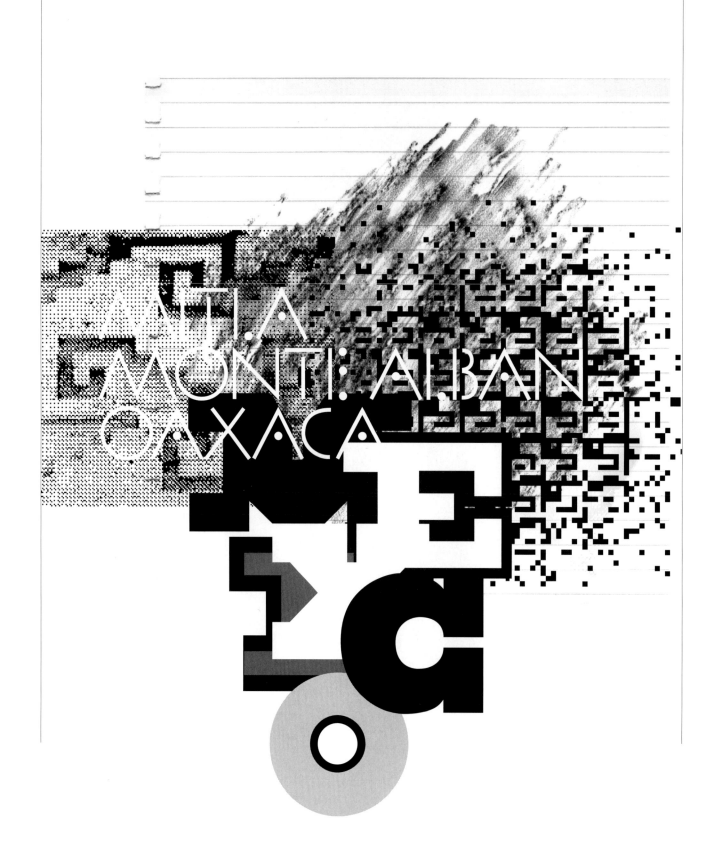

Theme:
**Range from drawing to construction**

| | | | |
|---|---|---|---|
| • | coarse | : | fine |
| • | loose | : | tight |
| • | random | : | patterned |
| • | amorphous | : | geometric |
| • | abstract | : | representational |
| • | flat | : | illusionary |

I wondered how dense a
textural overlap could be
and retain clarity.
I wondered how embedded
in texture words could be
without losing identity.

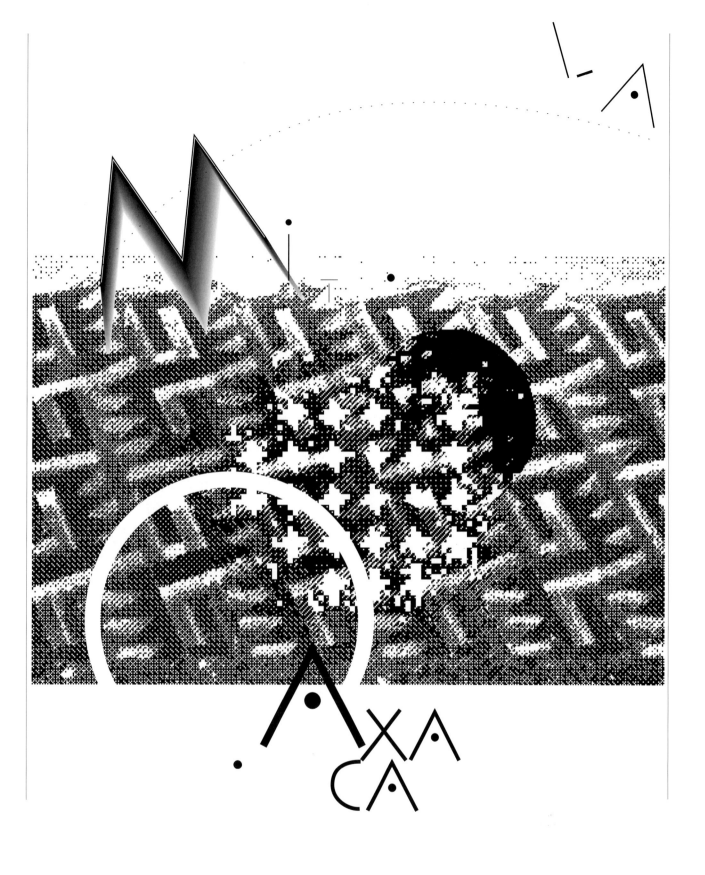

Theme:
**The stone mosaics of Mitla, astrological connotations**

| | | |
|---|---|---|
| • | coarse : | fine |
| • | loose : | tight |
| • | random : | patterned |
| | amorphous : | geometric |
| | abstract : | representational |
| • | flat : | illusionary |

I wondered whether or not texture could transform a physical site into a celestial arena, acknowledging the intense relationship of early Mesoamericans to the movements of stars and planets.

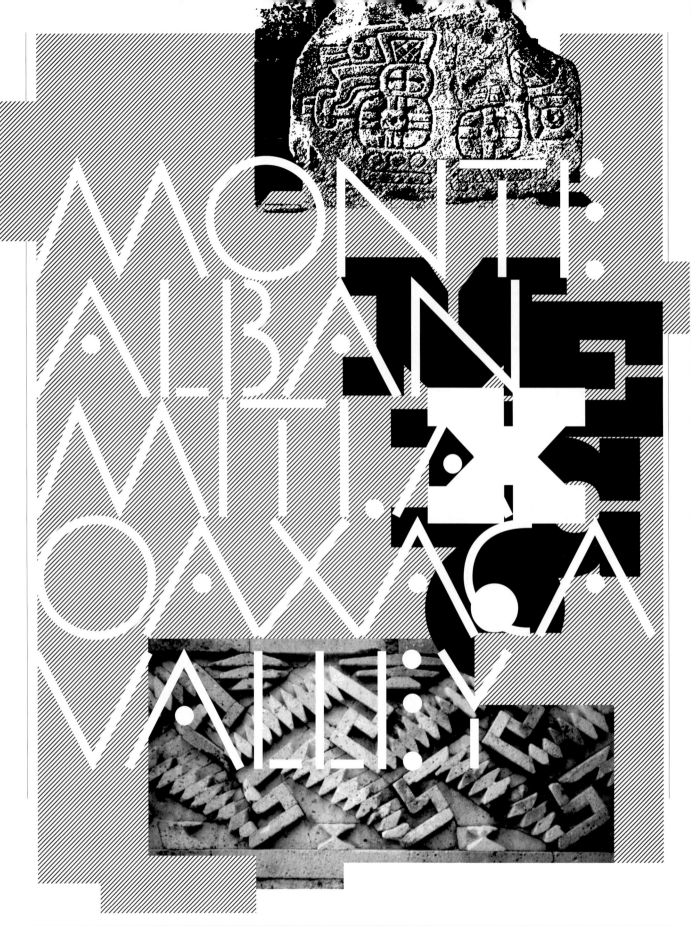

MONTE ALBAN MITLA OAXACA VALLEY

Theme:
**A Mixtec relief contrasted with a stone mosaic of Mitla; dominant letter structure**

|  | I | I |
|---|---|---|
| • | coarse : | fine |
|  | loose : | tight |
|  | random : | patterned |
| • | amorphous : | geometric |
|  | abstract : | representational |
|  | flat : | illusionary |

I wondered how coarse a structure could be and still be received texturally. I was interested in the way letter form edges were or were not affected by the background pattern.

**124**

# MITLA
## OAXACA
## VALLEY

Theme:
**A Mitla-inspired contemporary rug contrasted with a Mitla-inspired regular pattern and logotype**

| | | |
|---|---|---|
| • | coarse : | fine |
| | loose : | tight |
| | random : | patterned |
| • | amorphous : | geometric |
| • | abstract : | representational |
| | flat : | illusionary |

I wondered what degree of coarseness in the screen of the rug photograph would best convey its actual feel and how this texture could be made effective in a series of gradients from fine (in the logo) to coarse (in the larger pattern of the rug).

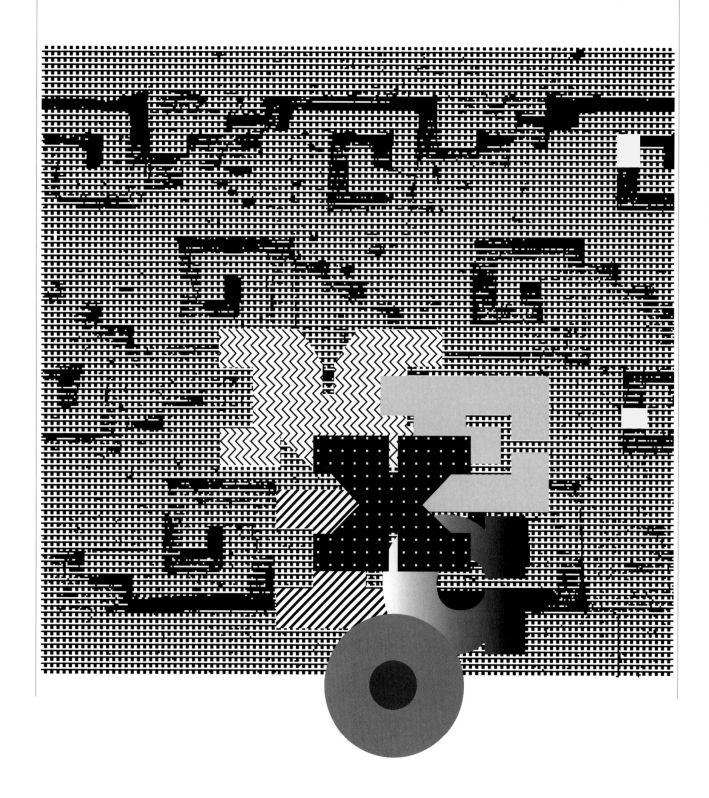

Theme:
**The stone mosaics of Mitla using patterned screen, combined with patterned logo**

| | | |
|---|---|---|
| • | coarse : | fine |
| | loose : | tight |
| • | random : | patterned |
| | amorphous : | geometric |
| • | abstract : | representational |
| | flat : | illusionary |

I wondered first if a time-ravaged ruin would be strengthened by a strongly assertive screen pattern designed to support the image, and then, could this highly textural image tolerate the implanting of additional textures of mainly similar gray value.

# OAXACA VALLEY

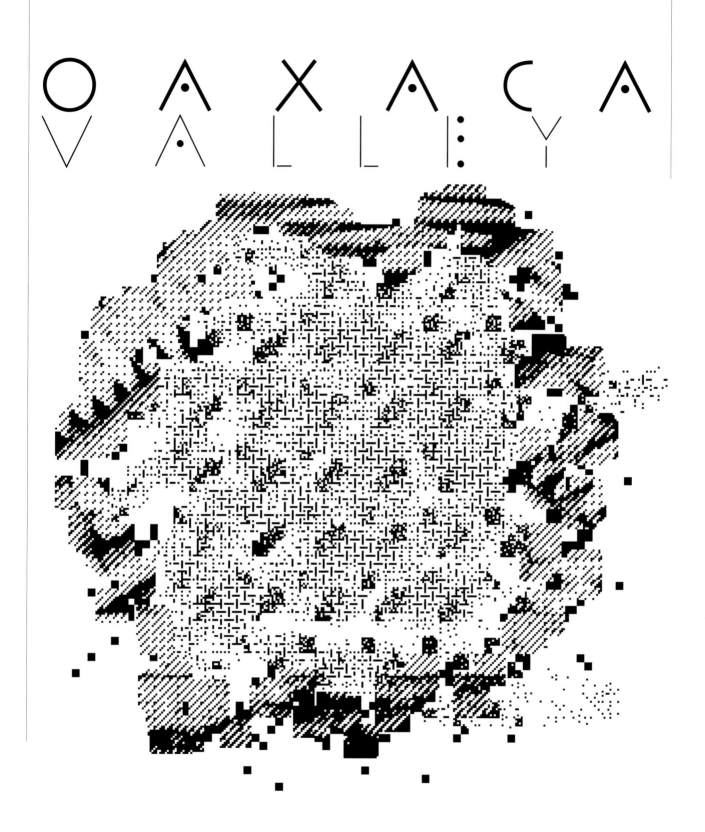

Theme:
**Superimposition of an eroded, derived pattern on an original Mitla pattern**

| | coarse | : | fine |
|---|---|---|---|
| • | loose | : | tight |
| • | random | : | patterned |
| • | amorphous | : | geometric |
| | abstract | : | representational |
| | flat | : | illusionary |

I wondered if one textural fragment could have enough variety in it to suggest depth and diversity.

OA
XA
CA

MONTI:
ALBAN

MI:
XI
CO

Theme:
**Step formations, Monte Albán**

|  | coarse | : | fine |
|---|---|---|---|
| • | loose | : | tight |
| • | random | : | patterned |
|  | amorphous | : | geometric |
| • | abstract | : | representational |
| • | flat | : | illusionary |

I wondered if digitizing a pencil drawing could give it a new authenticity, and if the coarse screening of a photograph would dramatize the erosion of the ruin while preserving the original majesty.

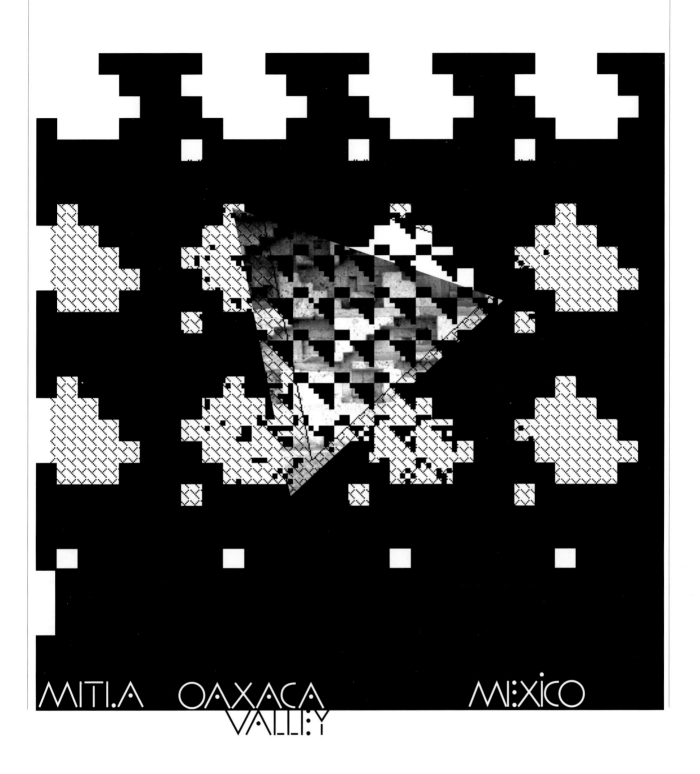

MITLA OAXACA VALLEY MEXICO

Theme:
**Derivations from the stone mosaics of Mitla**

Could larger shapes be
defined by smaller patterns
without losing either?

|   | | |
|---|---|---|
| • | coarse : | fine |
| | loose : | tight |
| • | random : | patterned |
| • | amorphous : | geometric |
| | abstract : | representational |
| • | flat : | illusionary |

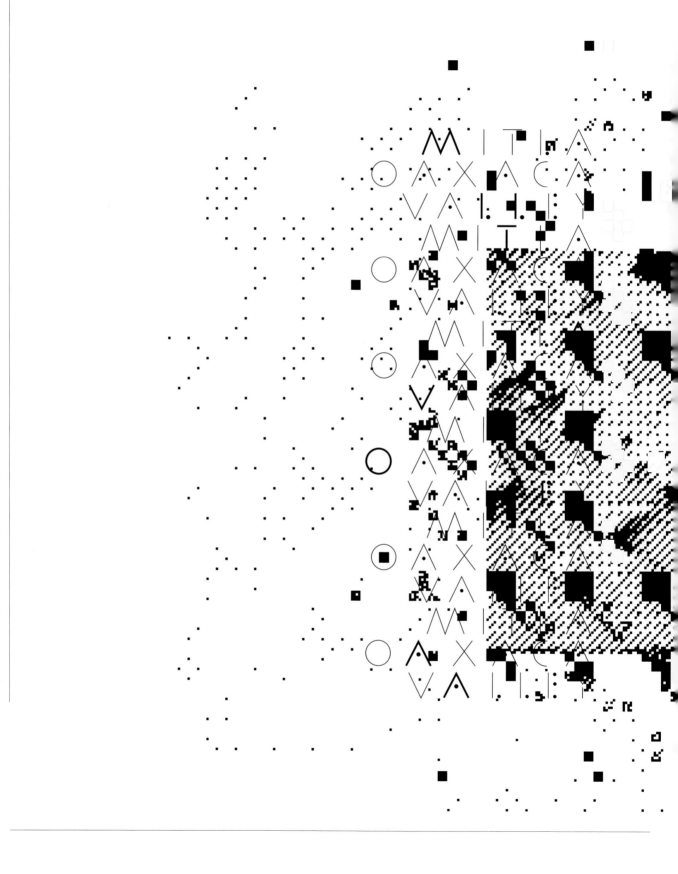

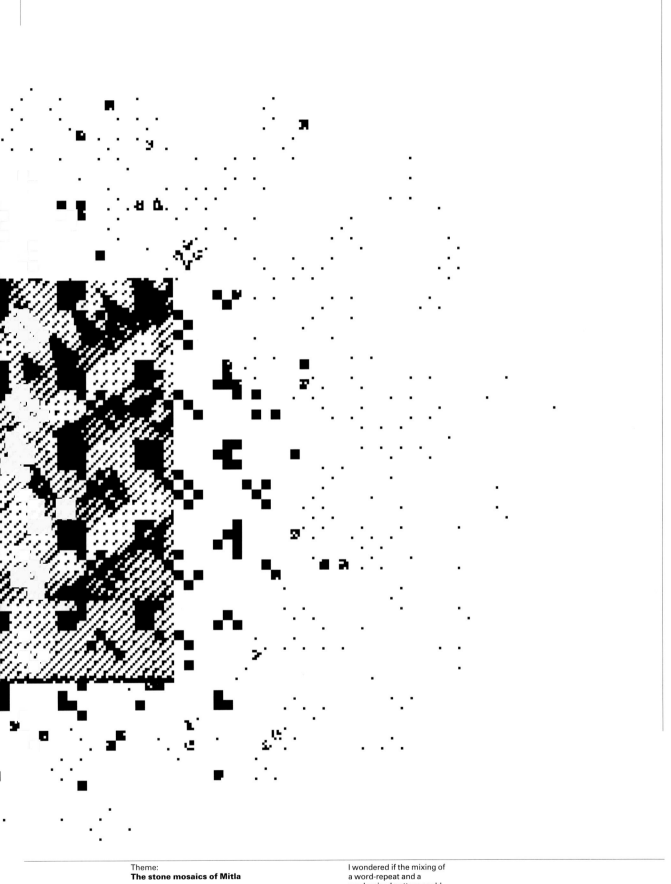

Theme:
**The stone mosaics of Mitla**

| | | |
|---|---|---|
| • | coarse : | fine |
| • | loose : | tight |
| • | random : | patterned |
| | amorphous : | geometric |
| | abstract : | representational |
| | flat : | illusionary |

I wondered if the mixing of a word-repeat and a randomized pattern could yield combinations that would add to the outward radiancy of the total image at the same time that a fresh interest in the words is created.

Theme:
**Guelaguetza—a traditional fiesta including frenzied dancing**

| | | |
|---|---|---|
| • | coarse : | fine |
| • | loose : | tight |
| • | random : | patterned |
| • | amorphous : | geometric |
| | abstract : | representational |
| • | flat : | illusionary |

Could the segmenting of this strange word be aided by defining changes of looseness and randomness between the parts? Could they convey at the same time a progression toward frenzy?

MONTE:
ALBÁN

M:XICO

OAXACA

Theme:
**Pyramid steps, Monte Albán**

|   |   |
|---|---|
| coarse : | fine |
| loose : | tight |
| random : | patterned |
| amorphous : | geometric |
| abstract : | representational |
| flat : | illusionary |

I was curious to know if depth-illusionary cues breaking the patterns of words could be a means of reconciling them to textural images in perspective.

ZO
-CA
-LO

OA
-XA
-CA

MI:
-XI
-CO

Theme:
**Street scene on the Zocalo (central square)**

| | | | |
|---|---|---|---|
| • | coarse | : | fine |
| • | loose | : | tight |
| • | random | : | patterned |
| • | amorphous | : | geometric |
| | abstract | : | representational |
| • | flat | : | illusionary |

I wondered how the three-syllable words could expand on the texture/pattern themes of the photograph and how the word structure could build on its vertical stress.

ZOCALO
OAXACA
MEXICO

Theme:
**Mitla-derived patterns used in a placemat motif,
concept by Eleanor Hiebert**

| | |
|---|---|
| • coarse | fine |
| • loose | tight |
| • random | patterned |
| • amorphous | geometric |
| • abstract | representational |
| • flat | illusionary |

I wondered if contrasting
texture could emphasize
the relation between
present-day Oaxaca and the
specter of its past hovering
over it.

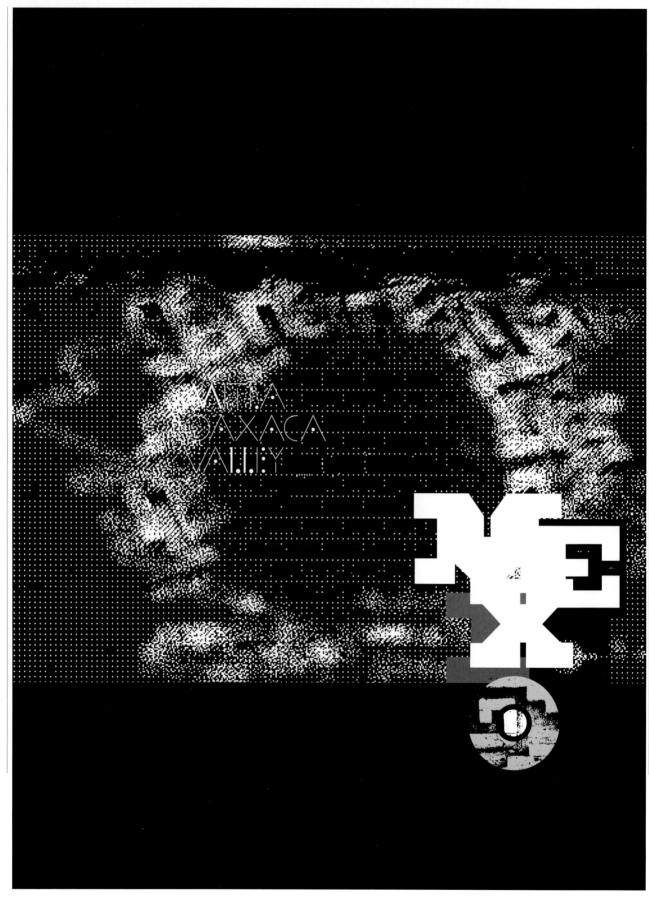

MITLA
OAXACA
VALLEY

Theme:
**The stone mosaics of Mitla, mystery**

| | coarse | : | fine |
|---|---|---|---|
| • | coarse | : | fine |
| • | loose | : | tight |
| • | random | : | patterned |
| • | amorphous | : | geometric |
| • | abstract | : | representational |
| • | flat | : | illusionary |

I wondered how far I could
go in dissolving the
diagonal stone relief motif
to create the obscure,
shadowy effect of night.

# 5.

Because of its emotional impact and because individual preferences are strong, color is a difficult subject to study objectively.

In this project, a structure for understanding color interaction is described and color terms are defined. Limiting color to a specific set (triad) establishes a base for an exploration of its basic qualities—hue, intensity, and lightness—and how they affect the interaction of color. Out of this exploration a unique color quality or resonance is progressively developed and applied to a series of posters.

The examples are by the author.

**• Technical Notes:**
Aldus Freehand® was used to generate all diagrams and examples.

## Goals:

To define an umbrella structure—the color sphere—that will accommodate the full range of pure color, that is, color not affected by other material qualities such as surface texture.

To define the key qualities of color.

To create an understanding of where any color is located within the larger structure and the directions in which it can be shifted.

To create an awareness of the variation potential of color in systematic terms.

To distinguish schematic from perceptual progressions of colors.

To apply a simple language of contrast (semantic differential) by which changes in any of the three basic color qualities can be observed:

hue (temperature):    warm—cool
intensity (saturation):  bright—muted
lightness (value):     light—dark

To use this vocabulary to describe the interaction among three specific colors of a triad.

To show the effect of changing any of the three qualities.

To show how quantitative contrast affects quality and communication.

To show the progressive application of a beginning triad to a communication in which form and color combine to create a specific, unique, integrated effect.

Process: See page 147.

"To be sure, we normally consider the absorption capacity of material to be its object color and we consider the spectral composition of radiation to be its light color. In reality, however, absorption capacity is only a latent ability and light rays are only information messengers that provide information, the way the postman delivers a letter. Color is only the product of the visual process, that is to say, color sensation . . . "
". . . the higher law of color theory is nothing—and cannot be anything—but the principle according to which the visual system functions. The law of vision is the basic law of color theory."
—Harald Kueppers

## The Relativity of Color

Reactions to color are very immediate and usually characterized by a decided like or dislike on the part of the viewer. Color, more than other aspects of design, is linked to personal taste—a vague sense of what "goes together," of "coordinates." This is not an adequate view of color for communication.

That color is an especially personal aspect of design is true. A special problem in education is to recognize personal sensitivity *while* building a self-critical attitude. Creating an objective base for the study of color is especially important and complex.

Besides the emotional-psychological aspect, there is the question as to whether viewers have a normally functioning visual system. This depends on the efficiency of each type of receptor in the retina—cones for each of the three additive primary colors, and rods which are sensitive primarily to the achromatic scale.

It would be of great value if, in the communication of color changes, there were a consensus on what it means to nudge a color warmer without changing either lightness or intensity, or to make it lighter without changing either hue or intensity. Since these qualities overlap and are easily confused, communication concerning color is often confusing.

What further confuses is that most people, unable to describe the retinal relativity of color, make a judgment based on association. Thus, a certain blue may be warm in relation to another blue but be categorically described as cold because of its association with water or sky or ice. We are surrounded by color labels based on association. Paint pigment color charts, by which considerable subtlety of color distinction is effectively communicated to the general public, use names such as apricot, brick, carnation, copper, forest green, melon, midnight, mulberry, seafoam, and thunder. Assuming there is something dependable in our common color awareness when we hear the word *melon* (watermelon, cantaloupe, honeydew, casawba?), how do we then speak of a modification? Should it be sweeter melon, blander melon, riper melon, greener melon? And what of the problem of the notorious unreliability of color memory?

As with other aspects of form, limitation is a way to focus the problem and clarify color qualities. It is also a way to open up an investigation of rich variation and uniqueness. Creating a more neutral base of numbered colors such as the Pantone Matching System (PMS®) or the Colorcurve® system takes color choice away from a fixed notion, describable by a name, and makes it variable with the direction of change describable by number. A numeric description does not, however, account for relative sensation—it is rather a means of specifying color objectively.

Clarifying the color qualities means clarifying the questions. When two colors are isolated, it is not so difficult to answer with consensus the simple, binary questions:

Which is warmer?
Which is brighter?
Which is lighter?

Reducing the choice to two color chips in a simple geometric shape, away from forms that could prompt associations, it is usually possible to agree.

The first question—which is warmer?—is not so difficult when the colors are far apart in the spectrum and of equal value, such as red and green. The complements yellow and violet present another difficulty: because they contrast in value, yellow, which might from a temperature standpoint be considered warmer, tends by its lightness to be cooler. Violet is cooler in temperature and warmer because of its darkness.

Also, a certain ambiguity occurs when colors are adjacent in the spectrum and are both within what is considered to be the key warm and cool zones of the spectrum. Thus, orange-red and red-orange tend to be ambiguously similar in warmth as are blue-green and green-blue in coldness. Of the three basic qualities, hue is also most prone to subjective associations which interfere with a more purely refined response, so that a correlation of hue with a cold object, as already observed, prevents one from seeing it as warm relative to another color.

The terms *hue*, *intensity*, and *lightness* and the terms used to describe the poles of contrast within each, are nontechnical words that are easy to remember. Warm/cool, bright/muted, light/dark are palpable, concrete descriptors that help—by virtue of their universality and their conceptual base—in making color application appropriate to content. The definition of color in these expressive terms takes away from a purely technical, mechanical approach.

### Color Context and Spirit

Color is unthinkable without form. A warm color presented in a hard geometric form, a cool color in a soft, diffuse form—these are ways in which opposing forces are used to keep qualities clear and effective. Hard/soft, rising/falling, close/far, central/peripheral—opposites give the context for the experience of color.

A color is made vibrant and effective by its context. Colors that in isolation may be dead, totally unappealing, can become spirited in the right color and form environment.

The word *spirit* in relation to color has a long history. We have developed connotations for the color representation of divine beings and divine qualities. Colors have come to be associated with emotional states. Colors are evoked by music. But color as a spiritual expression is predicated on the idea of relationship, and this must exclude much of contemporary color use in advertising and street graphics, in which color is used to separate, to pop out messages, to

violate both the plane in which it is presented and the uncorrupted, natural sensibilities of people. Born of insecurity about projecting in busy visual environments, commercial art resorts to outlines, creating backgrounds instead of spaces, thereby forcing the message. Fine artists of the modern movement— Albers, Braques, Klee, Morandi, Noland, for example—and artists of every time and culture have brought visual signs into dynamic relationship without resorting to these devices, demonstrating that form can be simultaneously assertive and beautifully integrated. Unfortunately, the computer makes distortion of form purely for the purpose of standing out in a composition easy and tempting for the untrained person as a way to embolden a message.

### Color Systems

The spirit of color can be negated by systems. Relying on systems for the definition of a color relationship can achieve a correct but lifeless effect, just as proper note-playing in music does not ensure a vital performance. The crucial factor of precise relationship may be missed. By operating on the basis of the *effect* of a found interaction, the painter and color master, Josef Albers, could separate himself from the dogma of the color wheel and its skewed lightness problem.

But Albers's method does not seem to get at the problem of mixing colors and knowing their location in the comprehensive color map—called here a color sphere—which his predecessors, but especially Ostwald and Munsell attempted. Itten, too, sees the value of systematic studies based on color harmonies—essentially symmetries derived from the color sphere—but mutates these in a more subjective way. Albers did not totally deny the usefulness of these theories, but he provided them as information after the empirical studies were completed.

The overview of color terminology presented here is a digest of terms and concepts that I have found useful personally and in my teaching. I was also pleased to see that they concurred with the structures developed by theorists of the past. I wanted to isolate those terms that I believe are useful in the designer's communication with himself, his peers, and production people. By presenting color terminology first and in sequence moving toward complexity, the linear thread from theory to application is perhaps most understandable. My own preference, however, based on my studies with an amazing perceptualist, Armin Hofmann, is for an intuitive search for the resonant interaction of colors first. Theoretical information then makes more sense when it serves to validate and explain an experience.

Similarly, in studying this material, it may be more instructive to start with the triads and examples on pages 148-158 before the theoretical introduction beginning on page 142.

**Color:**

Any specific color sensation produced by any one, or any combination, of six basic colors plus black and white.

Color is not a physical quality, but a sensation produced in the brain.

**Additive primary colors:**
**blue-violet (V), orange-red (O), green (G)**
(The alternate common designation RGB—red/green/blue—is less accurate in describing the sensitivity zones of the retina.)

These colors add by overlapping to produce lighter mixes; therefore all colors overlapping add up to white. The three additive primaries correspond to three types of receptors (cones) in the human retinal system.

The additive primaries are the primary colors of transmitted light, i.e., any system using light directly as the source, including TV, transparency projection, and, most important, the human visual system.

Black is the absence of light. White is the addition of all colors.

**Code to abbreviations for the primary colors:**

| | |
|---|---|
| Y | yellow |
| G | green |
| C | cyan |
| V | blue-violet |
| M | magenta |
| O | orange-red |
| | |
| W | white |
| B | black |

**The black-and-white diagrams distinguish among these colors in lightness only. The basic colors are distinctive enough to be imagined. Refer to the diagram on the back cover for colors that approximate the primary colors.**

**Subtractive primary colors:**
**cyan (C), magenta (M), yellow (Y)**

These colors overlap to produce darker mixes; therefore all colors overlapping produce black.

The subtractive primaries are the primary colors of reflected light, i.e., any system whereby color sensations are received by reflection from a surface, including printing on paper, painted or dyed surfaces—in other words, all colors mixed from pigments.

White is the absence of pigment, the subtraction of all color. Black is the addition of all colors.

**The subtractive and additive primaries isolated**

"The primary colors of transmitted light are the secondary colors of reflected light. Conversely, the primary colors of reflected light are the secondary colors of transmitted light."
—Canvas™ User Guide

*The cones in the retina of the eye do not see colors. They are collectors of quanta.*
*The three components of the visual system are the three [additive] primary colors.*
*A three-part code is formed for each color sensation. The primary colors are violet-blue, green, and orange-red.*
**—Harald Kueppers**

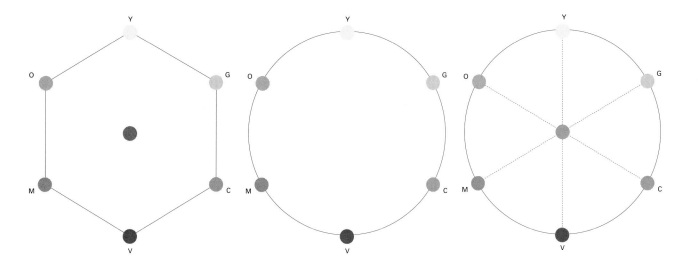

**Color hexagon:**
The combined additive and subtractive primaries.

**Color wheel:**
The full, continuous spectrum of colors presented in a circle, on which the primaries are key points.

**Complementary colors:**
Colors at opposite points of the color wheel which, when mixed in the correct proportion, yield a neutral gray. Complementaries assume both sets of primaries.

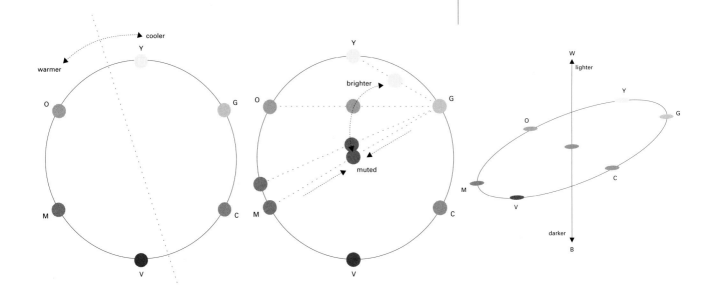

**Basic colors:**
The additive and subtractive primaries plus the achromatic colors black (B) and white (W).

**Hue scale: warm-cool**
The aspect of color determined by its wavelength and therefore its position on the color wheel perimeter. Also called chromaticity or temperature. A hue can be described as warmer or cooler in relation to another hue. (On the achromatic scale, white is generally considered to be cool; black is assumed to be warm.)

While the dotted line approximately divides the total spectrum into warm and cool sectors, it is also clear that from any point on the wheel, a color can be pushed toward warm or cool regardless of its position on the wheel.

**Intensity scale: bright-muted**
Describes the degree of purity (luminosity, saturation) of a color. Colors are subdued in intensity by mixing with other colors of the same value. A color of high intensity is saturated; a color of low intensity is muted. Maximum muting occurs when complements are mixed, near the center of the color wheel. Adjacent colors produce more intense mixtures.

**Lightness scale: light-dark**
The relative lightness or darkness of a color measured against a scale from white to black. Also called value. The pure colors of the spectrum vary in lightness. At peak intensity, yellow is closer to white, blue-violet is closer to black; therefore colors of equal intensity are not of equal lightness.

## The color sphere:

A comprehensive color structure reflects the interrelationship of the basic colors and the qualities of hue, intensity, and lightness. The color wheel is tilted to adjust for the lightness difference among the basic colors. The achromatic scale is embraced by a single central rod, analogous to the receptors for dark-light (rods) in the retina of the eye. To further compensate, the central rod is displaced to allow for more steps for the lighter colors.

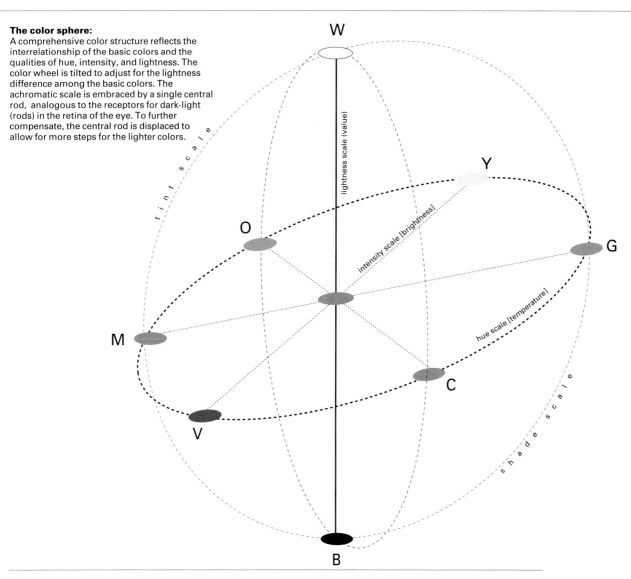

The number of colors possible by mixing is theoretically infinite and depends on how many steps are packed between the basic colors. Practically, a scale of 5 or 6 colors between the basic colors and white, black, or gray is adequate to show a substantial range of possibilities while making possible clear discrimination between steps, but the trained eye can discern much finer gradations so that a total color structure of 2,000 or more discrete colors is feasible.

The diagram shown would account for approximately 3,200 total steps if filled out in all directions. The tighter the packing of concentric rings in the color sphere, the greater the number of specific colors. The displaced center shows that there is more room for steps at the lighter side of the spectrum; that is, more steps would be perceptible there than on the darker side.

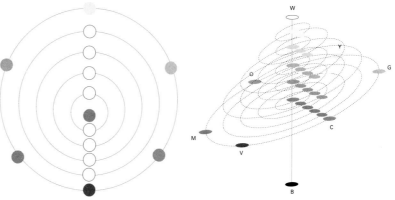

*"The number of terms in a scale will vary with artists and with the purposes of artists. . . . But the need for some scale . . . is constant. It remains fixed for all artists and for all purposes, for all men and styles of mind."*
—John F. A. Taylor

**Color scales:**
Progressions in which steps from one color to another are defined. Progressions take the form of systematic rows of colors. Tints and shades are one type of scale. Others cut through the color structure on unique paths.

**Tints:**
Tints allow the lightening of a color by adding white. In printing, screen tints allow the lightening of a color without adding another color. Percentages of tint screens in increments of 10% are arbitrary industry standards. Screen tint percentage steps corresponding to visual acuity, instead of arbitrary steps, are shown.

**Shades:**
Shades require the addition of black to create a scale of colors darker than the original color.

A progression contains effectively more steps at lighter values than at darker ones because the eye is more sensitive to change in the lighter range than the darker.

Mixing color from pigment means that substantially more pigment is required to make a visible step at darker values than at lighter ones.

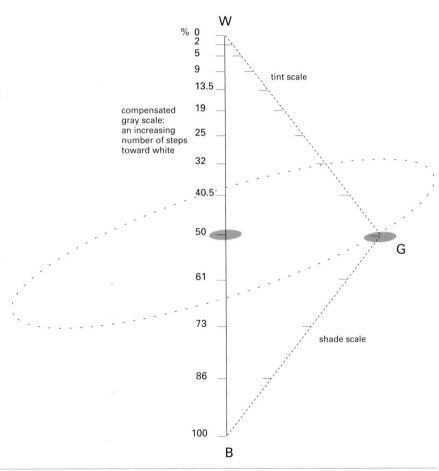

**Eccentric scales:**
Scales can intersect the color structure in any direction. Intervals can be in regular or geometric progression. A scale can be straight or curved.

Motion is the basis for a scale; a good scale has direction and no breaks in the flow of motion.

**a:** a scale begins as a tint of magenta and progresses in regular steps and on a straight line to a deep shade of violet.

**b:** a scale begins as a tint of yellow-green, spirals through gray to a muted violet in a geometric progression.

**c:** a scale beginning as an intense green-blue, arcs in regular steps through a mild tint and ends as a dark, muted version of the original color.

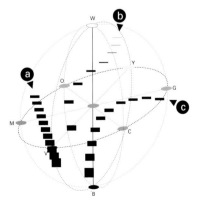

**Simultaneous contrast:**
The illusory sensation produced on the retina when the same color appears different in lightness, intensity, or temperature because of its relationship to other colors in the same configuration. It is most evident when lightness is similar. The eye tends to see two colors as dissimilarly as possible.

········ appears darker next to white

········ appears lighter next to black

**Successive contrast:**
The illusory sensation produced on the retina when, after first gazing at a color and then looking away, the complementary colors appear as an afterimage. Gaze at the three colors isolated in the black frame for 30 seconds. Then look at the black dot below. The complements to red and blue-green (green and orange-red) should appear as faint after-images.

**Finding lightness equivalence:**
It is difficult to establish equal lightness among colors of varying hue and intensity. Using standard tint scales and the binary questioning method (is this color darker or lighter than that color?), agreement can usually be reached.

Standard color scales such as the Pantone Matching System® are useful to make comparisons and achieve rough equivalence but are not reliable for systematic steps or final resolution.

Equating the lightness of colors at one level of a scale may not produce lightness equivalence at another. In Postscript® drawing programs, tints can usually be specified in any percentage.

The example above shows how lightness scales may vary within any given system. Finding lightness equivalence at one level usually means that other levels will not correspond.

**Gazing:**
The contrast effects are visible when the eyes are allowed to gaze at the color in a relaxed way and without focusing on any specific spot.

**"A number of studies in the field of psychology have verified the observation of Chevreul that colors look best (a) when they are closely related or analogous or (b) when they are complementary or in strong contrast. Analogous colors have an *emotional* quality, for they favor the warm or cool side of the spectrum . . . . Opposite or complementary colors have a *visual* quality, for they usually set a warm color against a cool one, thus causing a positive quality to offset a passive one."
--Faber Birren**

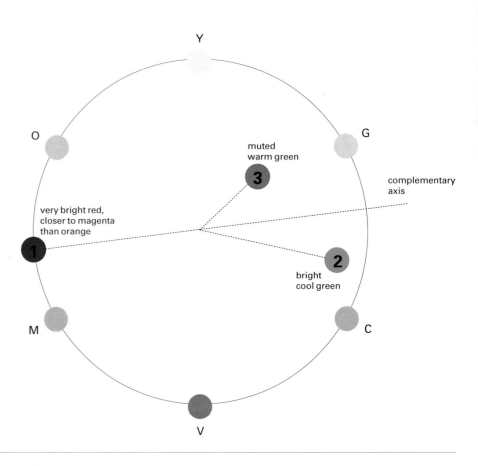

**Color chords:**
A color chord is a harmonic relationship, according to Johannes Itten. The four types of systematic chords are:
1. Dyads, or complements.
2. Triads, three hues whose positions on the color wheel form an equilateral triangle.
3. Tetrads, two pairs of complements with perpendicular axes to form a square, rectangle, or trapezoid.
4. Hexads, three pairs of complements.
The fundamental chords can be altered by changing any hue to a tint, shade, or gray dilution.

**Triads as defined for this project:**
Triad, as it is used in this chapter, refers to a set of three colors forming a unity rather than a strict definiton of three colors forming an equilateral triangle. They are formed out of a split-complementary relationship. In this relationship, one color is complementary to a pair of adjacent colors.
Triad A, page 148, can be described as shown above, where the complementary axis between green and red is split on the green side. The colors vary in intensity and are similar in value.

### Criteria for the universal/Unique poster

In this demonstration, a communication is the ultimate goal. Building from pure color is the best guarantee that the effectiveness of pure color will be preserved: it sets a high standard. But the criteria for a poster are additional ones. The following statement from the catalog to an actual exhibition titled "universal/Unique" gives the idea of the exhibition:

The title, "universal/Unique," is an encapsulation of one of the most fundamental concerns of human inquiry.

It reflects any of the following ideas:
- of the macro and the micro
- of the encompassing and the encompassed
- of the latent and the surface
- of background and foreground
- of pattern and disruption
- of archetype and interpretation
- of source and dénouement
- of society and the individual.

Rigorous training of thought involves the discipline of relationship between these poles.

The seminal impulses of modern design internationally have come from a discovery of the variation potential of elementary visual language when seen as an open system . . . a demonstration of the belief that by working within few but carefully conceived parameters, the number and quality of ideas and variations produced can be totally disproportionate to the apparent simplicity of the constraints. (This is, of course, the theme of this book of design demonstrations. It was, in fact, its inspiration.)

To be convincing the poster should demonstrate how a special quality is possible out of relatively few and universal elements; it should show a quality of movement toward uniqueness and complexity; many different possibilities should stem from the same beginning points. In summary, the posters should show uniqueness, movement, and variety.

---

**Process:**

Steps 1–5 are shown on the following three double-page spreads. Red and warm green are the constant colors of all three triads.

| 1 Triad selection | 2 Quantity contrast | 3 Lightness variations, three levels | 4 Lightness contrast variations | 5 Mixtures, gradations, patterns | 6 Five posters, universal/Unique, pages 154–58 |
|---|---|---|---|---|---|
| Triad A, pages 148–49: red plus warm and cool green | | | | | |
| Triad B, pages 150–51: red plus warm green and blue violet | | | | | |
| Triad C, pages 152–153 red plus warm green and cool red | | | | | |

---

**Note concerning the Macintosh® color cone:**

Seen schematically, the color structure of this computer is a cone standing on a black apex. White is its center at the level where the spectral colors are of lightest value and brightest intensity.

The diagram at right indicates approximately the distortion in lightness of the basic colors and white at maximum brightness of the Macintosh® color wheel. Whereas the colors vary drastically in intensity and lightness, they are shown as if in the same plane of lightness as at immediate right.

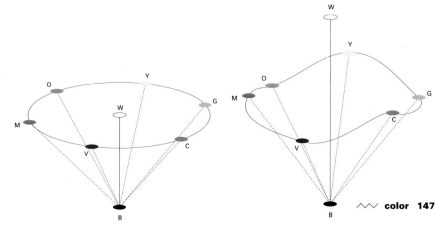

## Color Triads (Sets)

A set of colors, in this case a triad, can be described by breaking down the relationship into subsets. The basic subsets are hue, intensity and lightness.

Color interrelationship is enhanced when the subsets overlap. In this example, colors 1 and 3 are similar in being warm opposites to color 2, but colors 2 and 3 are similar in intensity compared to color 1. All three are similar in lightness. In each respect the grouping of colors varies so that any color is at the same time part of a different subset.

In this row,
each image
is composed of
elements of
approximately
equal lightness
▼

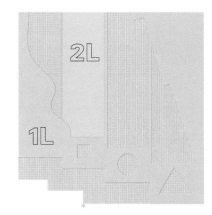

**Triad A:**

| | Intensity | Hue | Lightness |
|---|---|---|---|
| 1. red | bright | warm | equal |
| 2. blue-green | muted | cool | equal |
| 3. warm green | muted | warm | equal |

A dynamic
quantity
relationship
▼

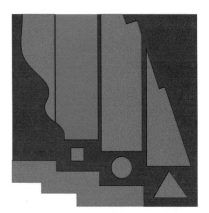

In this triad, the red (color 1), is in a split-complementary relationship to cool and warm green. Warm green (color 3) is muted and darkened to equate in value to red. Blue-green (color 2) is muted to a lesser, degree, bringing it closer to the perimeter of the wheel.
L=lighter; D=darker.

Mixtures of intensity,
lightness, temperature,
and pattern
▶

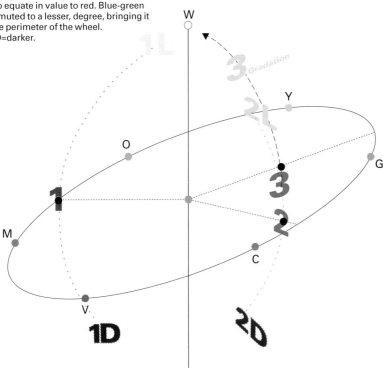

148

Achieving clarity with fewer elements is
preparation for greater complexity.
▼

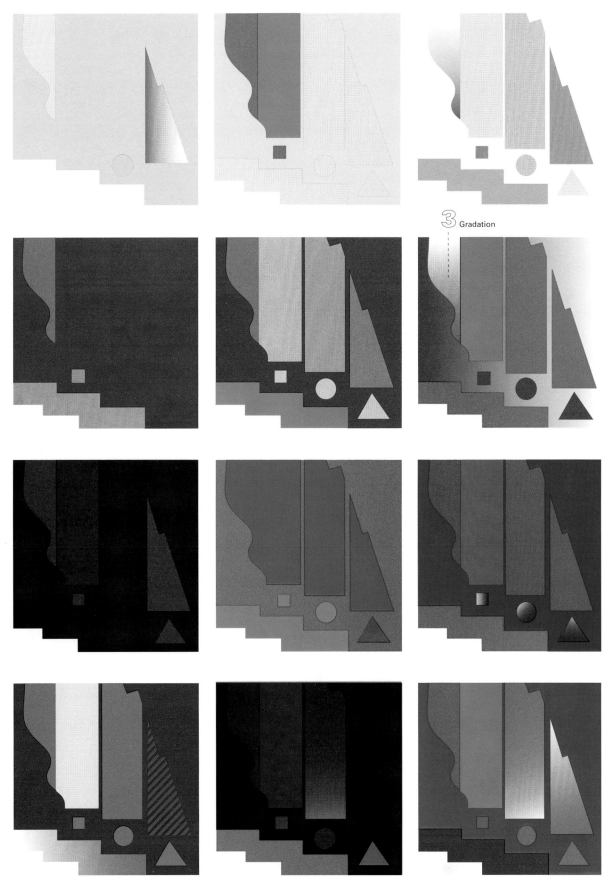

③ Gradation

In triads A, B, and C, red (color 1) and warm green (color 3) are identical. Color 2 moves around the wheel from adjacency to green to adjacency to red.

In this row, each image is composed of elements of approximately equal lightness
▼

**Triad B:**

| | Intensity | Hue | Lightness |
|---|---|---|---|
| 1. red | bright | warm | equal |
| 2. violet | bright | cool | equal |
| 3. warm green | muted | warm | equal |

A dynamic quantity relationship
▼

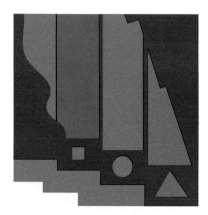

Compared to triad A, triad B shows a wide split-complement relationship of red in relation to warm green. The violet, color 2, has been lightened to be equivalent to red and warm green.

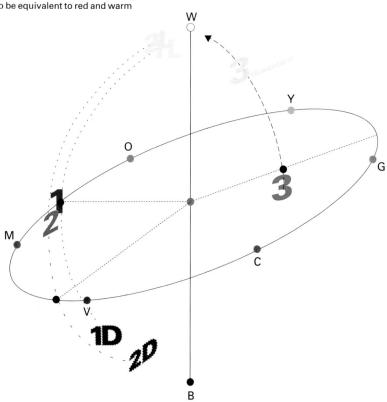

Mixtures of intensity, lightness, temperature, and pattern
▶

Achieving clarity with fewer elements is
preparation for greater complexity.
▼

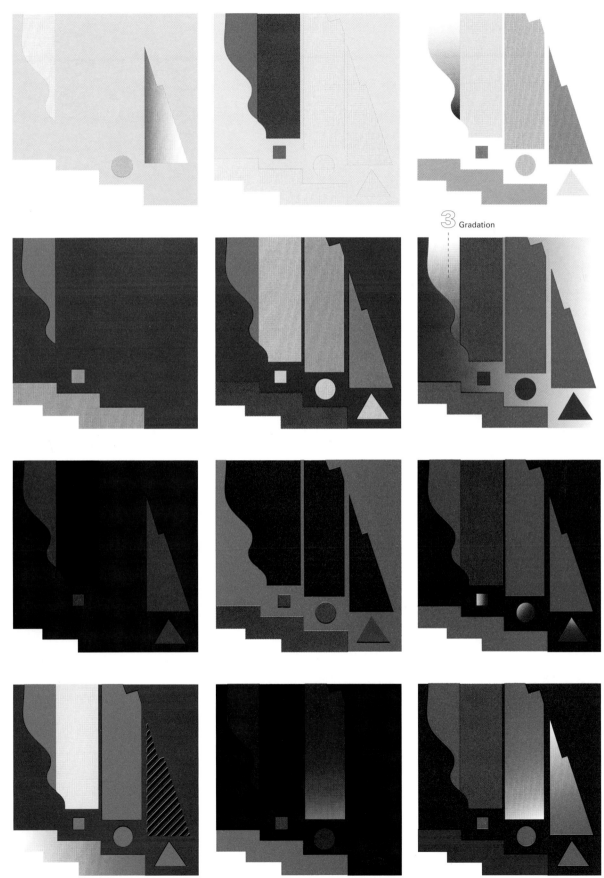

3 Gradation

The cool-warm contrast in this triad is subtler than in triads A and B.

In this row, each image is composed of elements of approximately equal lightness ▼

**Triad C:**

| | Intensity | Hue | Lightness |
|---|---|---|---|
| 1. warm red | bright | warm | equal |
| 2. cool red | bright | cool | equal |
| 3. warm green | muted | warm | equal |

A dynamic
quantity
relationship
▼

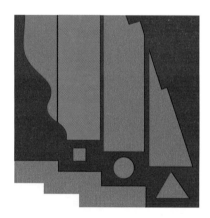

Compared to triad B, triad C shows a narrow split-complement relationship of red to warm green. Cool red, color 2, has been lightened slightly to be equivalent to red and warm green in value.

Mixtures of intensity,
lightness, temperature,
and pattern
▶

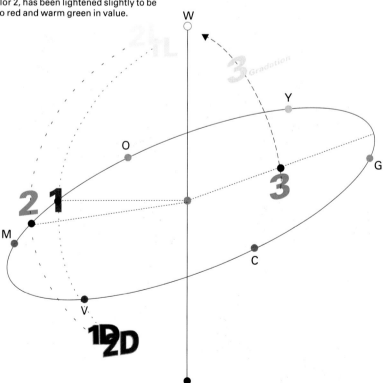

Achieving clarity with fewer elements is
preparation for greater complexity.
▼

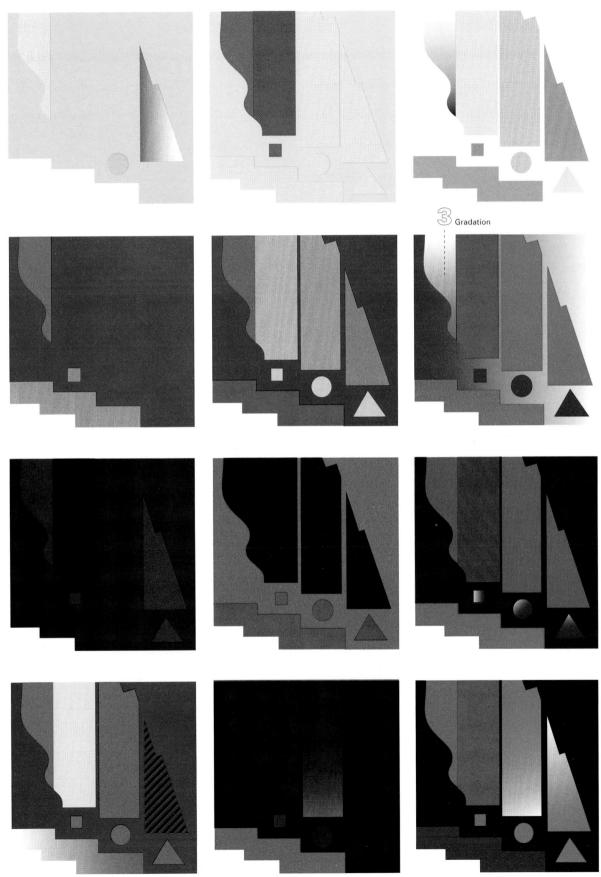

3 Gradation

Poster 1:
A progression from greater
to lesser lightness
employing tints and
warm-cool shifts.

universal
*Unique*

Poster 1:
A progression from greater
to lesser lightness
employing tints and
warm-cool shifts.

Poster 2:
A progression toward
lightness, brightness, and
linearity.

universal

unique

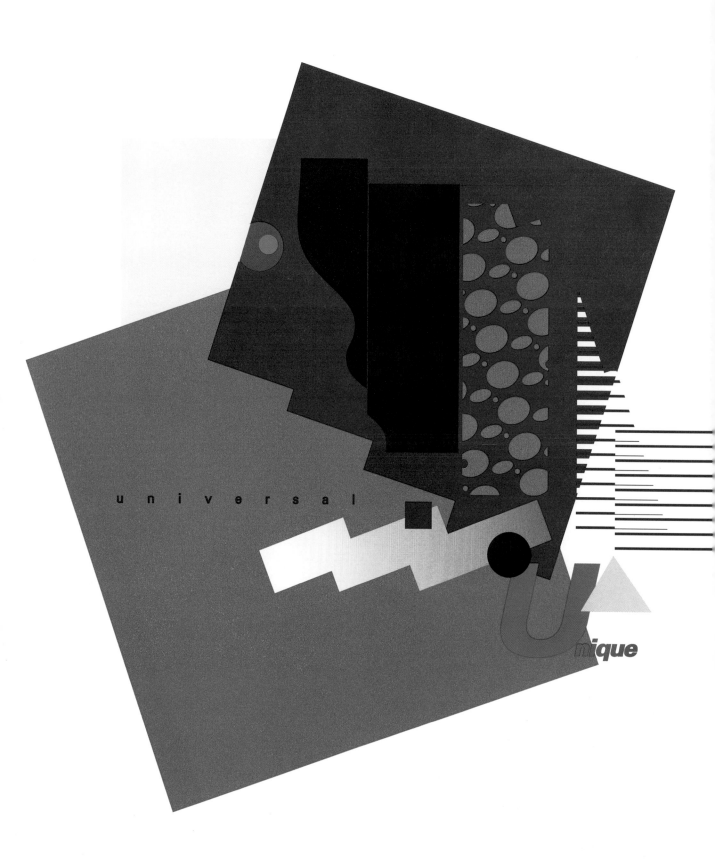

Poster 3:
The coolness of the
blue-green makes
everything else
effectively warm.
Quantity contrast makes
the blue-green active.

Poster 4:
Warm and cool interact
within a progression toward
lightness and increasing
complexity. "Universal" is
identified with a primary
color of high intensity;
"unique" is identified with
subtlety and nuance.

Poster 5:
A major contrast between
the cool, background,
universal square and the
warm, dynamic foreground
elements give the poster its
dominant character. Minor
shifts of hue, lightness, and
intensity add to the dynamic
quality.

universal

Unique

Project:          Double Analog Clocks

 **6.** *Creativity is characterized by the overlap or convergence of two otherwise unrelated ideas.*

*This project is a catalyst to challenge students to find a way to overlay ideas for characterizing a profession or vocation on an analog clock face of their own design. Three working clocks are made: a basic study clock and two clocks with vocational connotations. The clocks are named and an appropriate, simple logo designed. A package design completes the assignment.*

All examples are by students at The University of the Arts. The tools were conventional drawing, painting, cutting, pasting, and photographic tools on illustration board or other rigid surfaces.

**• Technical Notes:**
The basic clocks were converted in Illustrator 88® for presentation here. The clocks in color were photographed as 35mm transparencies by each student. The separations were scanned separately and stripped into pages formatted in PageMaker®.

"The mind has extended the views of the world
in a way of connecting everything with everything,
like God's eye (to take a theological point of view)
connects everything with everything . . . .
The moon has come in the reach of my grasp,
Then a lost shell somewhere at the bottom of the
Mediterranean
Can find its way to the notes, which daily I am writing.

"It is a sort of poetic trance, poetic transactions,
in which objects move into all directions,
from all directions,
everywhere.
The boundaries have disappeared—
this is what the Dadaists tried to make disappear . . . ."

—Stefan Wolpe

## Project 6 Summary:

### Goals:

*To achieve a fusion of two overlaid images in which each is also separately functional.*

*To synthesize syntactic, semantic, and pragmatic concerns in a project involving shape and dimensionality.*

### Process:

*1
As a one-day refresher project, design an analog clock with 10-inch diameter using elementary shapes to distinguish the clock hierarchy.*

*2
Propose three fields of human activity as possible subjects. In group discussion, select one that adds to the total range being studied in the class.*

*3
Research visual symbols and imagery appropriate to the chosen subject. Library research, on-site research, found images, photographs, drawings, drawing translations, and color studies are included. Contact with a specialist of the chosen field is encouraged.*

*4
Design two working double-analog clocks, that is, clocks with an analog face overlaid with an analogy to the subject chosen in step 2. A concept for the set of two is established; for example, serious/ crazy, abstract/concrete, visual/verbal, and so on.*

*5
Name the clocks. Look for a dual reference to time and the other subject. Use ordinary words if possible, avoiding acronyms. Use the chosen word as a basis to design a logo derived from existing type fonts. One logo applies to both clocks.*

*6
Construct the clocks, including the original study clock, as working clocks using a standard mechanism.*

*7
Package the clocks in a container that works structurally and visually with either clock.*

*picking out strands that fascinate us."*

**—Glenn Gould**

Document the project

Package the clocks

Basic design review: a minimalist analog clock

start

Design a time card and record time spent on this project

Propose three possible human activities for study; select one

Symbol research, visual experimentation

Begin final construction

12

Construct clock dummies

Define a logo:
—as a word
—as a visual device

Settle on two contrasting design approaches

**Process Diagram**

*The steps, and the relative time allocated, are summarized in the process diagram. (One hour on the diagram = one 6-hour studio session plus optional unsupervised time during the intervening week. Total project duration is twelve weeks.)*

Projects that deal with the overlay of apparently separate
things or ideas are especially important in education. Out
of this activity a basis for creating a matrix of meaning,
both for oneself and in one's work as a designer, is developed. Integrating aspects of great diversity, going beyond
collage or pastiche, is demanding, invigorating and
satisfying. The challenge to forge a unity between a
functioning clock and references to symbols of another
activity is an exercise in doing this.

Most of our daily experience comprises simultaneity of events
and stimuli to various senses. Out of these experiences,
amazingly, we are able to extract clarity if the *separate*
clarity of the events or stimuli is established.

The question for design is whether it can or should find a way
to present the complexity of experience. Is it possible to
deal with the intersections of diverse experiences and
create a unity out of them? Are we defeating the clarifying
purpose of communication if we layer information? Is
simple clarity really a delusion? Complexity can either
provide access to a purpose or distract from a purpose.

The clock project admits these questions. Requiring several
versions establishes a context within which a range from
simple to complex works as the criterion for each version.
How complex—that is, how richly diverse—can the
simple clock be? And how simply coherent in its overall
form can the complex versions be?

The project assumes that the issues dealt with in previous
chapters of this book have been understood, since the
success of complexity is dependent on the clarity of the
parts. This is important to note, inasmuch as usually—
given a choice—we opt for interest value of layered
constructions. Yet, without a progressive buildup of a
command of the elements of visual language, our desire is
unattainable. Once the more basic questions are resolved,
we are ready for layering.

Images carved in capitals of
columns in the Church of
St. Madeleine, Vezelay
(Burgundy), France, 12th–
13th century:
simultaneity of underlying
and overlaid forms.

In the opening stages especially, but also as refinement takes place, an openness to the possibilities presented by accidental juxtapositions and overlays is essential to the creative attitude. All this is in the interest of newness:
— new realities
— new perceptions
— new insights
— new intuitions
— new sensitivity
— new acuity
— new comprehension
— new knowledge
— new depth
— new wit
— new curiosity
— new incentives to learn
— new ways to communicate

The temptation is often to stop with the excitement of discovery before the material is digested and brought into refined relationship.

The double-analog clock project establishes an arena in which both discovery and resolution can occur. The clock face is first of all analog to the passage of time: it orients contextually, so we see time past and time coming. It is by now so universal a device that it is possible to orient oneself with two lines and a single "star." Reducing the clock to its minimal features can free the face for other treatment: this is the premise of the project. Because the elements are constantly being kinetically reconfigured, the resultant chance relationships keep the mind open and refreshed as the mixing of the clock and a counterform progresses. Change the time and you get instant feedback on how the elements work in different combinations.

First to consider is the question of the hierarchical clarity of the clock: the relative shape, size, and position of the hands and the dial markings. All of these are governed by norms, yet these are subject to reinterpretation in an internally relational system, for example, in the clocks for a TV news editor (pages 170-71), the second hand is not a "sweep-" style second hand but a smaller scale dial. The success of the clock's identity in relation to the overlaid subject depends on how well this *internally related* visual system as a set of shapes is resolved.

Secondly, there is the question of how well the overlay image set coheres in its own right. The forms must have their clear meaning beyond decoration and there must be criteria against which to evaluate the forms. In the visual realm much of our work is intuitive, yet the test is often in words. The flux between intuitive, formal search and verification through words gradually imbues meaning. One finds that a form hints at a meaning. The hint is then taken as a criterion which in turn is the means for strengthening the statement into a less personal and hidden form.

The morphologies suggested in previous chapters are all observable in these more complex projects. Their function is to place a formal-structural aspect within a verbally stated contrast set. In this project, key words specific to the respective topics are used as added criteria. I learned the technique of writing down key words from Armin Hofmann. It is a way to set up a control mechanism in advance of sketching a form. In practice, a lot of words are furnished in marketing briefs; these may or may not be useful for developing visual form. Wittingly or not, words are often used to conceal or mask an object's real character. Consequently many forms in commercial graphics are borrowed from whatever stylistic trend may prevail. Thus instead of adding to visual language, commercial applications can easily have the effect of wearing down, of depleting language.

The kind of words used has a great bearing on subsequent development. Some words easily confuse and muddle our thinking. A reductive approach which tries for essences is the one taken here. The words may seem simplistic and coarse; they are for this reason most useful. Refinement and adjustment of nuances is the function of the visualization.

In the displays that follow, a list of key words, thought to have strong visual connotations, is included. An abstract concept such as *caring* does not have an immediate visual connotation, but words like *holding* or *encompassing*, which are close to *embracing*, do.

Since one of the primary goals in communication is to create memorability, and since motion—as has been discussed in chapter 2— is significant to memory, verbs have been listed first, descriptive modifiers (adjectives, adverbs) second, and nouns last. The breakdown into grammatical components is only for purposes of questioning and analysis. In a completed visualization, several aspects are fused into a "sentence" of actions, descriptors, and subjects.

**"The eye sees noun and verb as one; things in motion, motion in things, and so the Chinese conception tends to represent them. 'Rice-field' plus 'struggle'=male. 'Boat plus water,' boat water, a ripple."**
**—Ernest Fenellosa**

**Study clock**

Explores the relationship between two large but passive dots, representing the clock's face and the home position of 12, and a set of three precise, floating, dynamic triangles.

# Magnitude

▲
**Logo**

Besides the obvious progression in size as it relates to the word *magnitude*, the Bodoni typeface relates on a second level by its shift in stroke weight.

**Clock 1**　　　　▶

Research on the relation of the clock integers to concepts or modes of representation in other languages and cultures yielded a set of substitutions.

**Key words:**

| v. | adj.-adv. | n. |
|---|---|---|
| calculate | analytic | cipher |
| quantify | cerebral | code |
| relate | precise | equation |
| theorize | | factor |
| | | group |
| | | interval |
| | | numeral |

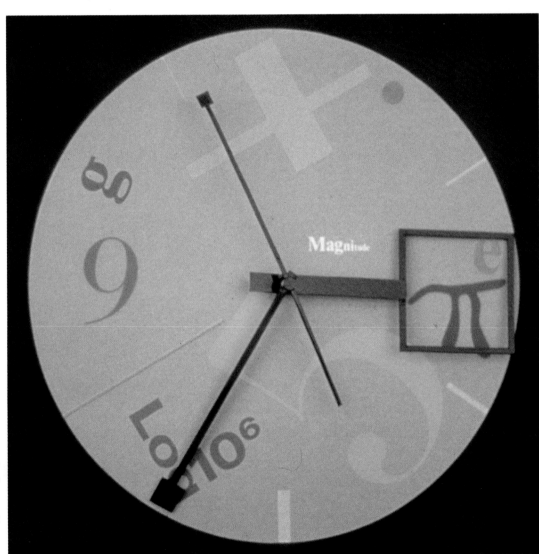

**Clock 2** ▶

A mix of literal and
equivalent mathemati-
cal symbols in
contrasting size convert
otherwise verbal
symbols to strongly
visual and colorful
forms. The hour hand is
like a magnifier with
the other hands
repeating and varying
its form.

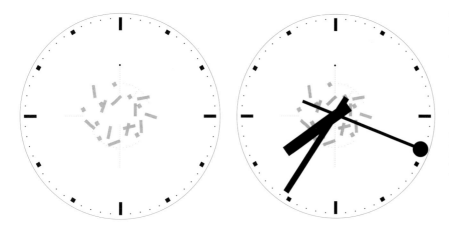

**Study clock**

The hierarchical relationship among three categories of minute markers is explored. The same marks are used to form an antiphonal, chaotic center. The cipherlike hands reinforce the chaos in their overlap at the center and at the same time the clarity of the dial as they reach toward it.

**track**

▲

**Logo**

Explores the degree to which letter forms can be cancelled with simultaneous increase in *effective* legibility.

**Clock 1**          ▶

In the clocks for a trainmaster, the idea of the study clock is used in a specific way. The hands are clear, signal-like extensions from a cluster of overlapped railroad signs. The logo travels with the second hand. Four different track notation types are used to divide the face into logical quadrants. The sense of order comes from the way several signs out of many become meaningful and clear.

**Key words:**

| v. | adj.-adv. | n. |
|---|---|---|
| control | accurate | signal |
| direct | clear | light |
| warn | secure | gauge |
| | | location |

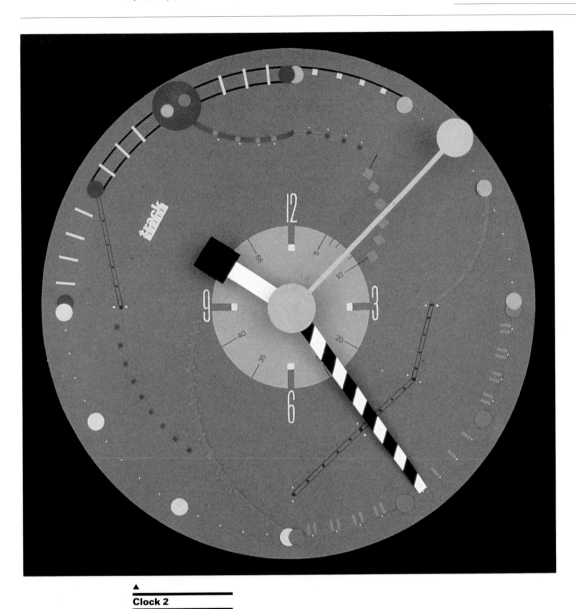

▲

## Clock 2

The second clock is an inversion of the first, in which a free distribution of colorful, track-like rhythms is placed in the outer zone. The signal-like hands reach out from a precise and ordered center, conveying a sense of control.

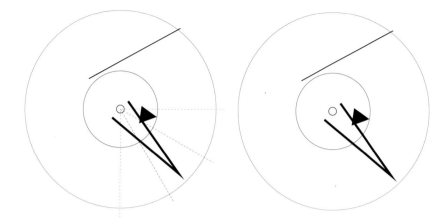

Formulating the hands as arrows and wand sets the stage for maintaining clarity in a complex image and finding equivalents from human lore in the applied versions. The visual speed of the hands corresponds to the speed of their movement. The eccentric second hand presses forward by its diagonal action.

# evolv-
# ing

▲

## Logo

The logo suggests progression in the left-to-right movement and mutation in the baseline shift. The letter spacing is normal; the uniqueness comes from the interlock of the two lines.

## Clock 1 ▶

A timeline identifying the stages of human development is organized as a circular diagram replacing the numerals and using the increments of the clock to represent the approximate relative duration of the stages. In searching for visual elements that would emphasize this historical evolution, the skull seemed appropriate as a static image corresponding to the static face of the clock. The astronaut, floating in space, represents the reach of present-day man—he floats weightlessly as the hour hand moves through its cycle. For a brief time, at about 3:00, the image locks in with the skull, from which it is partly derived. In its overall form, the hour hand resembles a human hand. The spear as second hand and the combination male-female symbol as minute hand combine with the hour hand to create a set showing a range of abstract symbolism: concrete to symbolic to literal.

Key words:

| v. | adj.-adv. | n. |
|---|---|---|
| collect | cultural | contexts |
| compare | diverse | objects |
| decipher | historical | relationships |
| measure | | patterns |
| | | societies |
| | | succession |

▲
**Clock 2**

The varied faces of humankind becoming the face of the clock had to be developed as a sufficiently continuous texture to avoid losing the hands. The collage is black and white; the hands are bright color. The evolutionary stages are marked abstractly and in color on the perimeter of the clock.

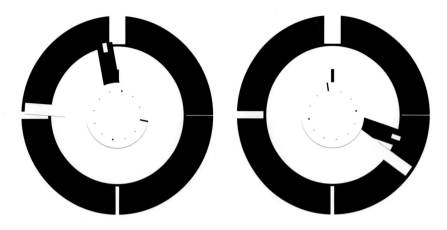

### Study clock

A coarse outer dial is contrasted with a fine, rotating seconds dial. The progression from a fine 3:00 marking to a bold 12:00 marking is symbolic of advancing time.

# current

▲

### Logo

*Current* is a word referring to the flow of things, to current events in this case. The only letter rendered unclear by the strike-through is the letter *e*. This situation is used to advantage by substituting an abstract bar. Dynamic placement of the bar adds to the overall effect and makes a connection to the idea of selection and editing by isolating an "event."

### Clock 1                   ▶

A free and nebulous drawing is used to represent a world of unpredictability. By contrast, the hands—derived from the study clock—are simple and massive. As the editor extracts and clarifies stories from myriad events, the hands are in a sense moments of clarity within a vast arena.

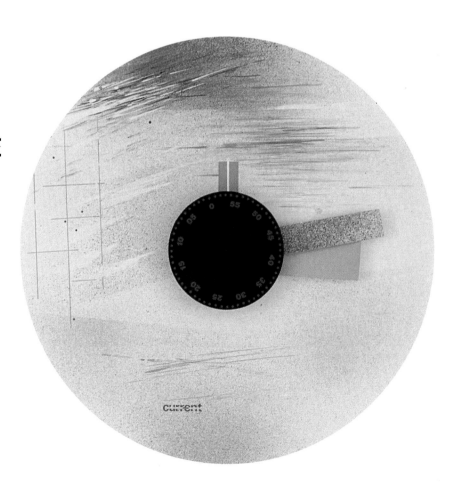

## Clocks
## for a
## TV News Editor

design and photography
by Robert Hovsepian

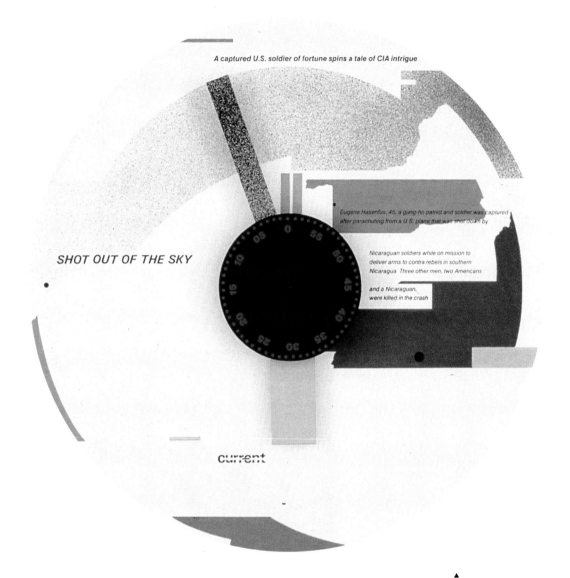

A captured U.S. soldier of fortune spins a tale of CIA intrigue

SHOT OUT OF THE SKY

Eugene Hasenfus, 45, a gung-ho patriot and soldier was captured after parachuting from a U.S. plane that was shot down by

Nicaraguan soldiers while on mission to deliver arms to contra rebels in southern Nicaragua. Three other men, two Americans

and a Nicaraguan, were killed in the crash

current

▲
**Clock 2**

Specific episodes from
news of a given day are
isolated—"edited"—
and placed against
the nebulous field of
clock 1.

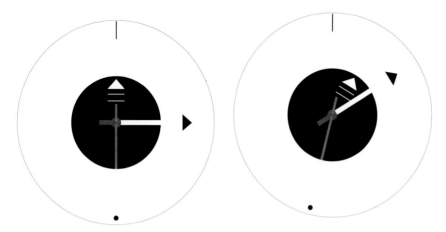

**Study clock**

The relationship of a center from which elements extend into an outer zone lays the basis for clocks with added specific content. (The version at left does not show a logical time situation; it shows only the relative iconic character of the hands.)

▲
**Logo**

Sift—sort—sand—time: the key ingredients of the logo concept. The parts vary in arrangement as shown on the clocks.

**Clock 1** ▶

With modern art as a theme, a collage is created in the center from which several "artifacts," appropriate to the clock face, emerge as selections.

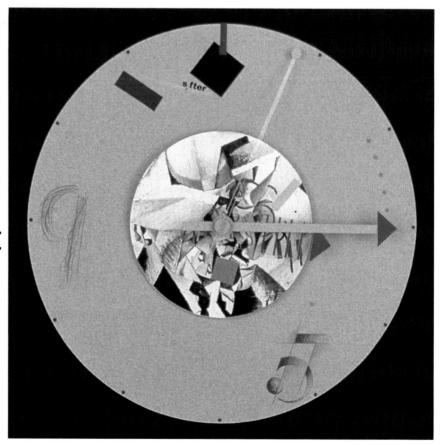

**Key words:**

| v. | adj.-adv. | n. |
|---|---|---|
| arrange | discerning | archive |
| classify | keen | gallery |
| cull | sensitive | |
| evaluate | | |
| filter | | |
| inform | | |
| screen | | |
| show | | |

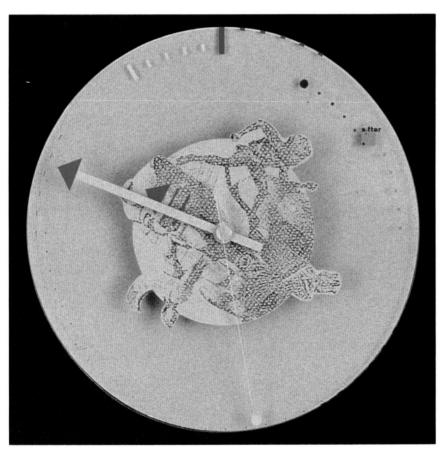

**◄ Clock 2**

The central collage is changed to combine classical, historical artifacts into a central core or criterion against which the sorting, sifting activity of the curator occurs.

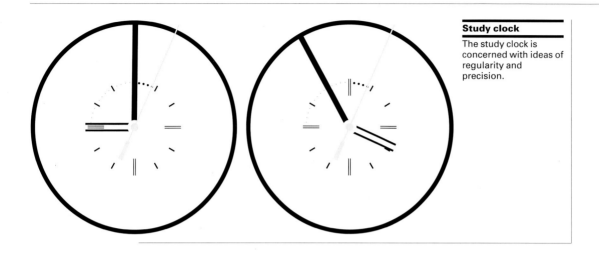

**Study clock**

The study clock is concerned with ideas of regularity and precision.

# PULSE

▲
**Logo**

A simple statement of a regular beat.

**Clock 1** ▶

The use of an exact formal language augmented by the familiar image of the geometric cross reinforce the idea of dependability conveyed by the alternating, regular beat of "PULSE."

**Clock 2** ▶

In contrast, the face suggests the chaos and pressure against which the nurse works.

**Key words:**

| v. | adj.-adv. | n. |
|---|---|---|
| assure | alert | bandage |
| care | dependable | charts |
| protect | sensitive | pulse |
| | | wound |

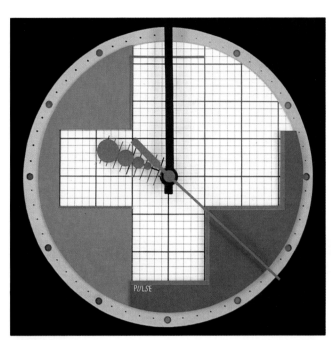

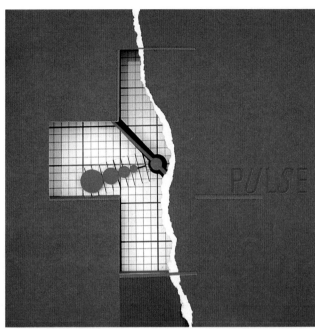

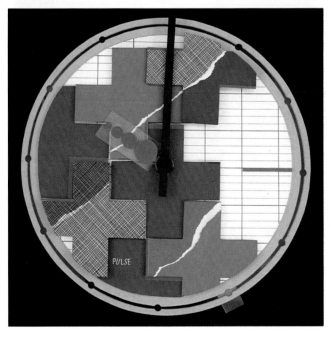

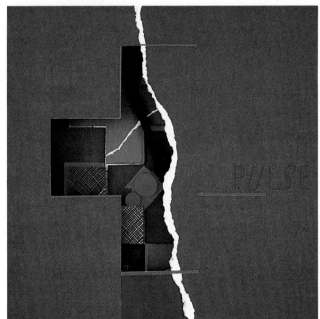

The package has a
window which reveals
the substantial
difference between the
two clocks.

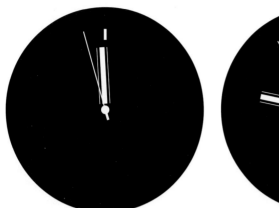

## Study clock

A minimal clock structure consisting of lines of varying length lays the basis for the applied clocks.

# Timeline ►

▲
## Logo

The regularity of the normal spacing of the letters, as well as the mono-weighted type style emphasizes the linear character of the word *timeline*, which has an obvious connection to both the clock and the work of an archeologist.

## Clock 1 ►

The question is whether a technical diagram, related to the clock by its circular features, can be presented without interfering with the latent diagram of the clock by which time is read. The diagram is recognizably of Stonehenge, the classical ancient structure in England.

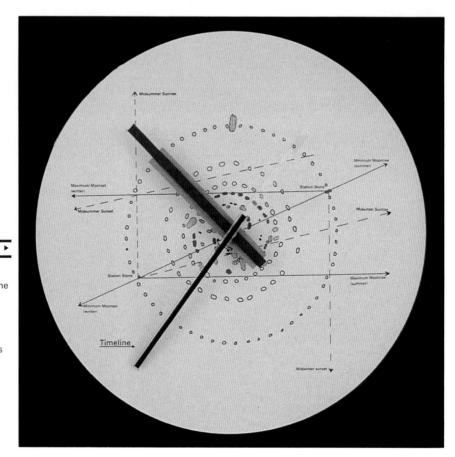

**Clocks**

**for an**

**Archeologist**

design and photography
by Ellen J. Schneider

**Key words:**

| v. | adj.-adv. | n. |
|---|---|---|
| analyze | fragmented | history |
| dig | unfamiliar | puzzle |
| probe | mysterious | ruin |
| reconstruct | distant | |
| speculate | | |

**◄ Clock 2**

A *dig* is the basis for a
playful clock in which
another classical
archeological subject,
an Easter Island head
sculpture, is lost and
dug out of "terrain" of
the same color and
texture.

By combining
elements from both
clocks in a random
way, the incoherence
of found historical
objects in a ruinous
state is suggested on
the package.

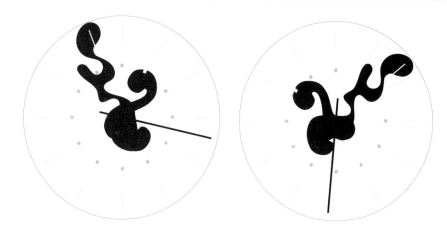

An investigation to see if relatively random, amorphous forms could work as sufficiently precise indicators and how much support would be required from the structure of the dial. The amorphous forms were changed to angular ones after the investment theme was adopted.

### Logo

EFEX=Foreign Exchange. A time and movement connotation is achieved in the abstract treatment of *E*. The letters read with or without the vowels. An acronym seems appropriate for an international corporate subject.

### Clock 1 ▶

An investigation of the relation of world market currencies and their relative time zones led to creating a dial which travels with the hour hand to reflect these. The hour marker can be placed in any of the zones to establish it as a base. The global inference is emphasized by the bleeding of diverse paper currencies off the edge.

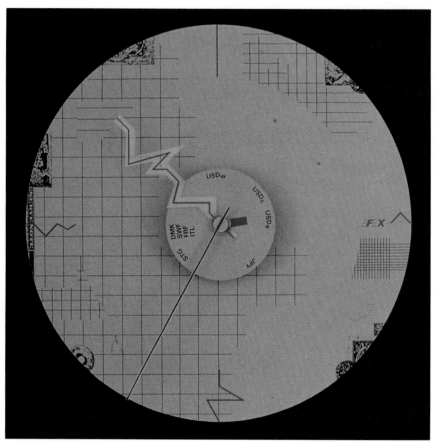

**Key words:**

| v. | adj.-adv. | n. |
|---|---|---|
| calculate | erratic | broker |
| forecast | cyclical | global |
| parlay | | investments |
| | | intermediary |

**◄ Clock 2**

The essential structure
of clock 1 is retained in
a dimensional version
for which the erratic
undulations of the
market are the basis.
The resulting
concentric arcs convey
a sense of cyclical ups
and downs.

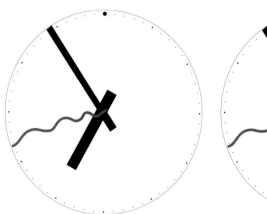
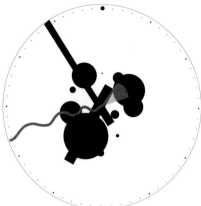

**Study clock**

A wavy second hand
and random dot motif
in the center set the
tone for a whimsical
subject.

## ON THE AIR
## OFF THE AIR

▲

### Logo

The flux between being
on and off the air is a
way to characterize the
life of a disc jockey.
The alignment of the
repetitive segments of
the two phrases
emphasizes the
contrast between on
and off. On and off are
primary functions
representing the
dichotomy active/
inactive, connected/
disconnected, alert/
passive.

### Clock 1 ▶

"On the Air" is about a
changing mix of music,
talk, news, and
commercials. A base of
concentric rings
alludes to spinning
discs. Irregular wedges
of music and words are
played against this
base. The minute and
hour hands follow the
wedge theme, the hour
hand solid, the minute
hand "noisier." The
overlay of hands and
face at different times
produces unpredict-
able combinations; the
use of red to mark the
key edges or points of
the hands allows the
time to be read through
the complex visual
structure.

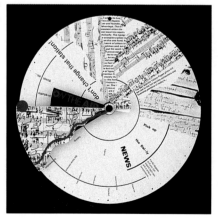

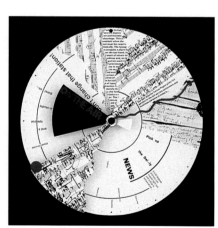

design and photography
by Mark Sylvester

| **Key words:** | *v.* | *adj.-adv.* | *n.* |
|---|---|---|---|
| | mix | lively | rhythm |
| | sequence | relaxing | texture |
| | spin | spontaneous | variety |

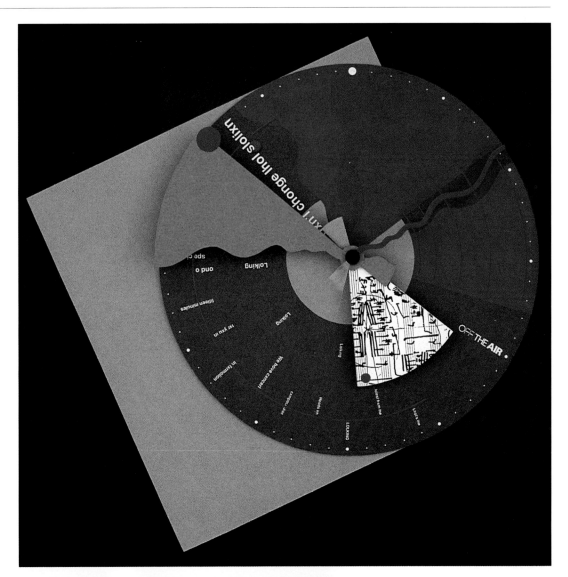

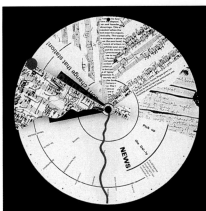

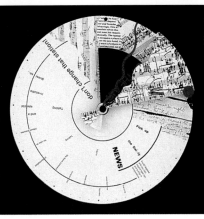

▲

## Clock 2

"Off the Air" replaces
most of the verbiage
and visual noise
with color. Whereas
clock 1 is constant
communication, clock
2 is intentional non-
communication.  A
background panel
pivots out to suggest
the record sleeve. The
angle reference
contributes to a sense
of casualness.

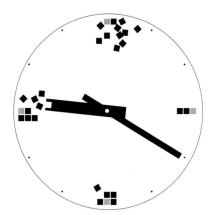

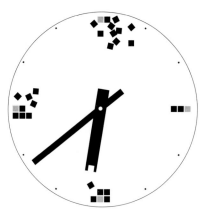

### Study clock

The progressive breaking up and restoring of a tight modular cluster is the theme of the study clock. The idea of combining a firm directional quality with a dissolution the strict order of the clock face is pursued in a totally different way in the sign painter's clocks.

# Sign
# -Age

### Logo

The logo is a play on a word for architectural graphics. In the hyphenated form a connection to the time theme is found. The flush right arrangement adds to the unity of the lower case letters and emphasizes the uniqueness of the capitals.

### Clock 1 ▶

A research of lettering styles from simple to decorative preceded the development of a set of five elements placed in size and stylistic progression. The outer contour of the face is shaped by cutting out the number 2, a reference to three-dimensional qualities of signage.

**Key words:**

| v. | adj.-adv. | n. |
|---|---|---|
| adapt | attractive | alignments |
| clarify | clear | decoration |
| cut | colorful | direction |
| paint | versatile | numbers |
| point | | words |
| | | symbols |

▲
**Clock 2**

The process of painting dummy models of clock 1 left residues of paint strokes on scrap-paper used as back-drop. Because the random brush strokes were in themselves attractive and suggestive of a larger process range from sketch to refined finish, the second clock incorporates them in its design. The round face is suggested against a square field by a masking process similar to that experienced in painting over an element on paper, then removing the element.

### Study clock

Eccentricity, creating a moving "shadow," is explored as a way to create a sense of visible change through the day. The hour hand is carried by a moving disk with a displaced center.

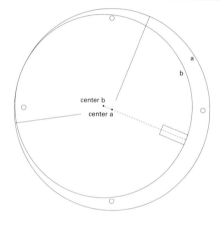

center b
center a

a
b

▲

### Logo

The subject of these clocks is the effect of the changing length of daylight hours through the year in the temperate zone and its effect on the propagation of plants. The otherwise prosaic name "Light Time" is made more effective by the size change and the use of letter weight and background gradations. A connection to the clock theme is made clearer, too.

### Clock 1 ◀

A diagram showing the change in available natural light in the course of the year comprises the context for a small-scale clock in which the principle of the study clock is used to express the dark–light shift through the day. The clock reminds the botanist that passing time substantially affects the growing season of plants.

### Clock 2 ▶

In this version the diagram is replaced with a foliage photograph with a dark–light shift. The connection is a formal one.

**Clocks**

**for a**

**Botanist**

design and photography
by Chris Wise

**Key words:**

| v. | adj.-adv. | n. |
|---|---|---|
| calibrate | cyclical | life |
| cultivate | discerning | light |
| observe | responsive | plant |
| plan | anticipatory | root |
| plant | | seed |
| predict | | soil |

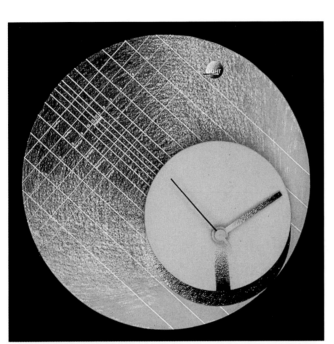

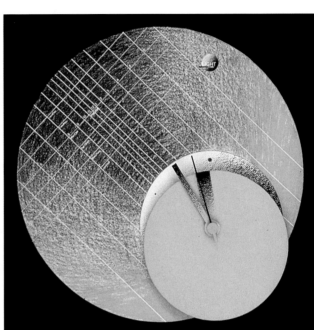

**Clock with Package**

The face of a mirror,
the hands derived from
the tools of the trade,
the logo playing on
the dual reference to
the clock face and the
human face, the
package incorporating
references to the hair,
the mirror, and the
logo. An example of
using clichés of a trade
to solve the problem
uniquely.

# 7.

*Graphic images presented over time is the subject of this project. A logotype designed for a museum is the basis. A morphology of changes in form and movement and a modular notational system for scoring animation sequences are developed.*

*(Assembled sequences in color are presented on a disk obtainable separately as a supplement to the book.)*

All examples are by the author.

**• Technical Notes:**
Sequences were prepared in MacroMind Director®, with paint images imported in part from other drawing programs, including video scans using MacVision® and processed in Hypercard®. To order a disk containing these examples, send $10 to:

KH Graphics / GDP
7731 Mill Road
Elkins Park, PA  19117

The disk includes the MacroMind Director® player module. It requires an 8-bit color monitor and is available in Macintosh format only. Users may duplicate the disk freely. The disk also includes the font DotLineCaps.

**Project 7 Summary:**

### Goals:

**to maintain a strong and persistent logo identity in a series of spot TV announcement prototypes.**

**to use characteristics of motion and color change in relation to specific criteria (key words).**

**to see rhythm in time as an extension of rhythm in space.**

**to see how slowing down processes of metamorphosis that are often too hurried can yield a deeper and more satisfying experience.**

**to explore techniques to get greater than usual viewer involvement in image completion.**

**to understand the casting and scoring processes of a multimedia computer program.**

**to develop and apply a simple morphology to describe features of graphics in time.**

**to develop a general use scoring method for scripting basic animation sequences.**

**Process: See page 198.**

"Subjective time seems to be determined more by the density of an event and our involvement in it than by its progression—the relative clock-time duration of the event . . . . The more involved we are in the event, the shorter it seems. The less involved we are, the longer it seems, . . . the subjective time during a waiting period seems to stretch endlessly."
—Herbert Zettl

This project brings together all the previous themes—space, sign-symbol, word/image, texture::pattern, color, and overlay—and adds the dimension of time to a simple subject. To show the results requires a medium other than print. A computer disk, which is available separately, shows moving sequences in color on a properly equipped computer monitor. These examples are required to make this chapter fully meaningful.

When it comes to inherent interest, moving images have the edge, independent of image quality. Even with still images, such as those shown in previous chapters, the criterion for interest is a kinetic quality of movement among the sets and subsets of a composition. "Static" is a pejorative for visual images intended for visual communication.

A still image and a moving image each have their cycles, the time of "reading" required to take them in. But rarely does a viewer take enough time to fully process a still image. A moving image, by comparison, suggests we haven't seen it all as long as new motion is taking place and tends to force us through cycles. Moving images take a more totalitarian grip on the viewer and demand to be seen to completion; pages of a book cannot do this.

Because of the transfixing quality of moving images, entertainment easily supersedes communication. The swooping, distorting, intersecting, multiplanar logos of commercial television are symptomatic of the desperate attempts of networks to hold audience. And the absurdly twisting scoring tables and player statistics of sports broadcasting suggest that the motion of the sport itself is not enough to hold an audience conditioned to incessant motion during the stale moments of waiting, which are part of any sports event. Entrancing computer graphics keep people glued to their sets. From a purely visual standpoint, the commercials are often more dynamic than the sports action.

It is interesting that even television can benefit from the refreshing use of a single, straightforward type face. With no "tricks" of presentation, simplicity is an antidote to the excesses of overdone graphics. The pendulum swings as saturation is reached. Rather than following the trends and countertrends, it is most useful to know the range from

Right, an excerpt from the score for *Sequenza III,* for solo soprano voice, by Luciano Berio. The score uses a graphic notation language to express motion and direction, and words to convey the feeling. "Tense muttering" followed by "distant and dreamy" create an indelible contrast that gives a very clear criterion for performance.

**Books are not Movies!**

If you page through a book, you have the options of skimming or thoroughly processing or something in between.

This can be a kinetic event. But imagine a book whose pages are turned by some mysterious and immutable hand, whether you are already finished and waiting or haven't

had time to get it all. It's hard to imagine that the same timing could work for more than even one person. Two people, each reading a text in silence, will rarely

finish at the same time. It seems amazing that in the realm of visual sequencing it is possible to arrive at timing sequences that are supposedly right for vast

numbers of people. Or does this suggest that in adjusting to mass audiences, other subtler, more contemplation-inviting sequences are essentially neglected?

simple to complex and to be able to apply an approach appropriately—to be able to inject at any time a clear signal into the environment in which a graphic is supposed to get attention.

In this chapter we ask the question, what permission or opening does specific content give to the formulation of kinetic events, and how can this combat the kind of entropy inherent in the repetition of stock effects?

The informational part of the chapter consists of an orientation to a basic morphology of form and motion coupled to symbols that can be handwritten with relative ease. A structure is then suggested for representing kinetic events in time and interrelationship.

### Kinesthetics, Human Rhythm, and Perception

The at-rest human heartbeat of 65-72 beats per minute is a natural and important point of reference to which we can all relate. A *second* is a close enough standard time reference. Our perception of the duration of a second is dependent on many factors. A successful kinetic sequence transports us so that we lose a sense of how much time has gone by.

Film and video are ephemeral media; the experience is fleeting. Nothing is left when it is over except an impression. Their usefulness is therefore primarily to create an impression and to create emotional attachment. Inherently as media— aside from the ways they are actually often used—film and video tend to lend themselves, therefore, to some subject matter or processes more than others.

Like music, visual animation on a video or computer screen happens in a single space. Even though there is a succession of images which might be presented as linear in a score—as it is in music—the experience is actually a series of replacements in the same space. The succession of images leaves a short trail in memory, enough to carry continuity.

In film, continuity is made firstly by the filmmaker's sequencing of individual frames (the basic unit of film) and secondly by the eye's bridging the momentary blanks between frames by means of retinally created afterimages.

The basic unit of computer animation and television is the entire, constantly pulsing image. We speak of frames in video or computer animation as a matter of convenience in creating steps of a progression, even though frames as such are not a property of the medium.

### The Structure of Scores

• Scores and Channels

A score is a diagram using mainly abstract symbols to represent the interrelationship of parts of an event. The scoring method suggested here is based on a primary channel for the form and motion of each cast member and the stage, with two narrower secondary channels for rhythm and color. As in musical scores, where multiple staffs of five lines are usually necessary, here multiple channels are stacked to show the parallel and simultaneous events.

In music it is possible to follow a score: one watches the evolution of music on a sheet of paper. If notation of a visual evolution is effective, there should be a clear correlation between the written score and the visual sequence as it appears on screen.

However, there is a problem in scoring a visual event as compared to scoring music. In visual animation we use the same sense organs to view the event as are being used to observe the score. This means that there will always be an interruption in the performance when one refers to the score.

But are scores prescriptions or sketches? More typically, a score for an animation is not an absolutely precise document to ensure relatively similar performances in different places with different performers. It is primarily useful as a reference sketch for working out sequences in a one-time environment. So it is actually more suggestive of events, centers, and time frames than it is absolutely prescriptive. At best it is a point of departure to get a handle on a concept, a way to define an intention before confronting the additional complexity of instructions to a computer.

It is preposterous to think, at this time in history when even musical notation has departed radically from its traditional

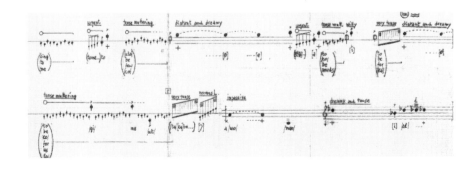

conventions, that a universal scoring method for kinesthetic events could be found.

The purpose in this chapter is to show how one can build up a notational structure which is appropriate to one's own way of working.

## • Symbolic Notation

Symbolic notation is a shorthand method of bringing complex events into a single field in order to visualize their interrelationship. Symbols are useful to the extent that they can accurately describe a form or event, can be used with relative speed and convenience, and if they provide objectivity that enables communication of concept and structure, especially in settings involving other technologies and where other persons are involved.

The 26-letter alphabet with its upper-case variations, numerals, and punctuation gives us a symbol set large enough to form any verbal thought. Variation comes through combination.

Like the written alphabet, the idea of a modular approach in developing the scoring language for animation is to create a limited, learnable set of symbols, supported by mnemonics. To keep the total number of symbols small, formal or movement functions are indicated by attaching modifiers. We can do this either by combining symbols, or, where more practical, by adding verbal notations or inserting more detailed sketches, as is done with conventional illustration-oriented, storyboard presentations.

## • The Stage

Think of the screen as a stage. It is the field within which the action takes place. Color and other visual characteristics are programmed in a channel reserved for the stage.

## • Cast Members

A cast member is the smallest unit having its own independent activity. Normally, each cast member occupies its own channel in the score. A score will expand or contract in vertical depth depending on how many cast members are "on stage." This is roughly equivalent to providing one

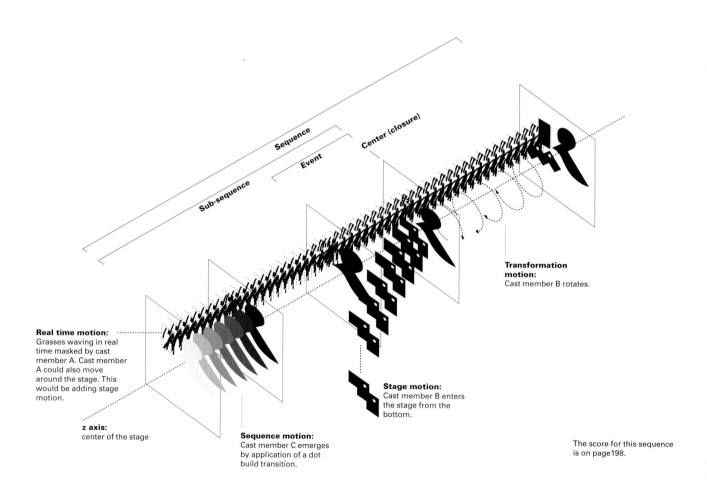

**Sequence**

**Sub-sequence**

**Event**

**Center (closure)**

**Transformation motion:**
Cast member B rotates.

**Real time motion:**
Grasses waving in real time masked by cast member A. Cast member A could also move around the stage. This would be adding stage motion.

**Stage motion:**
Cast member B enters the stage from the bottom.

**z axis:**
center of the stage

**Sequence motion:**
Cast member C emerges by application of a dot build transition.

The score for this sequence is on page198.

staff for each instrument or voice in a musical score.

- **Types of Motion**
- —*Real time motion* is the motion of an object or person as it actually occurs, such as grasses waving or a person dancing. A real time sequence is treated as a "movie" and as a whole can function as one cast member.
- —*Stage motion* refers to the movement of a cast member on the screen as an act of design.
- —*Transformational motion* refers to the way a cast member undergoes a change in form such as becoming amorphous or filling with a pattern.
- —*Sequence motion* refers to the connecting transitions between events. These are typically stock transitional devices, such as dissolves and fades, in which speed and direction of change can be controlled.

The studies shown in this chapter concentrate on stage motion. They are based on programming as an act of design.

- **Vectors as Motion Indicators**

A vector is an indicator of direction. An image or object can, by its form, point in a direction—a chimney, for example, points up. This is called a *graphic vector*. If the image or object points unmistakably to something—an arrow, for instance—this is called an *index vector*. Graphic and index vectors are both properties of the image and not of their path across the screen. The path across the screen is a *motion vector*.

Every part of a sequence has its own motion vector. The more vectors (of color, form, sound) that point in the same direction, the more closure and predictability of perception is gained. Sound is often used to create closure when visual closure is weak. By closure we mean the coming to a culmination and clarification of a form or event.

- **Sequences, Events, Centers, and Closure**

It is useful to see sequences hierarchically as comprised of events and centers.

An *event* consists in the appearance, transformation, and exit or dissolve of a cast member or a group of cast members. A *center* occurs when the actions of multiple cast members culminate an event, unifying the action, and thus create a moment of *closure*.

In conventional storyboards that describe the succession of centers—the landmark changes in a *sequence*—not much attention is given to the event surrounding the center. An event is summarized as "cut to" or "dissolve to" without reference to other qualities of the transitional event itself. The intention behind such minimizing is to play down what are considered to be only effects in relation to the principal action. Can these effects become a more integral part of the primary image action by making them part of the meaning rather than just embellishment?

- **Sound**

Music, voice, or other sound would typically be added to visual animation. In the scoring approach described here, it is assumed that the following approaches could work:

1. The sound track is structured separately and placed as a whole in a separate track without specific reference to events. In this case it functions as a blanket to assist in creating closure for the whole sequence.
2. The sound is designed with its own cast members in much the same way that the visual score is designed; it uses the visual score as a prompt.
3. A visual score is developed in response to an existing sound score.

Visual sequencing is the primary concern of this chapter; sound is not explored.

### Conceptual Scores vs Execution Scores

In a program such as that used to create the demonstrations for this chapter (MacroMind Director®), the score in general is managed in a way analogous to the method offered here. However, separate windows (for defining the visual character of forms, cast members, text, and sequencing) and the limited size of windows on the screen break up the score so that it is difficult to proceed without a conceptual map that shows the total shape of the score. While MacroMind Director® (MMD) is relatively simple to use with practice, it is easy to fall into a pattern of reacting to

"The 'classical' films or any other pieces of art resist entropy (running down) because they carry a universal message (form and content) that is not easily rendered useless by contextual change."
—Herbert Zettl

the surprises offered by the computer and the software. This is certainly one way to work—and one which I have encouraged throughout this book—and to learn about the possibilities, but it is less useful for defining a time-specific concept with specific communication goals.

It should be emphasized that a conceptual scoring approach in no way offers an introduction to the use of any specific animation or multimedia program. Rather it is a tool that can function as a preliminary to working in *any* program while attempting by the symbol language to anticipate, and not confuse with, symbols and language typically used in software programs. Naturally, the symbol language can be modified to conform to specific symbols of a software program.

The examples offered on the separate disk can be viewed with the player module furnished on the disk. They can also be opened in the full MMD program to see how the score is worked out in detail. *Please note that the disk does not contain software for the production of scores for animation.*

### Footnote on the Limitations of a Medium

The smoothness, speed, and color range of animated transformations will depend on equipment and software sophistication and memory availability.

The low-end software chosen for this demonstration is limited in sophistication but adequate to show the transformations in principle and within the limitations of popular hardware configurations. (I should add that the capabilities of the program used have by no means been exploited to the greatest possible degree of sophistication or complexity.) All software programs are being constantly upgraded; the programming features that are now a part of MacroMind Director® add a level of potential not exploited in the examples prepared prior to the most recent release. In any case, it is not really possible—nor desirable—to keep abreast of high-end electronic technology at the beginning instructional level. The concern of this chapter is more with a way of *scoring* animation. This is a technique that can be applied at any level, and elaborated by designers in a way appropriate to their needs.

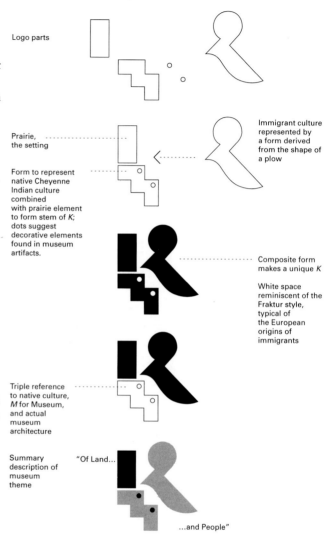

Logo parts

Prairie, the setting

Form to represent native Cheyenne Indian culture combined with prairie element to form stem of *K*; dots suggest decorative elements found in museum artifacts.

Triple reference to native culture, *M* for Museum, and actual museum architecture

Summary description of museum theme

"Of Land...

...and People"

Immigrant culture represented by a form derived from the shape of a plow

Composite form makes a unique *K*

White space reminiscent of the Fraktur style, typical of the European origins of immigrants

The logo used as a subject was designed for the Kauffman Museum, a museum of the American prairie featuring the natural and human ecology of the plains. The primary subjects are the prairie, agricultural cultivation, the Native American culture of the region, and an immigrant culture as an overlay to the pre-existing natural and social environments.

| Types of Movement and Change (syntax) | Museum Key Words (meaning) | | | |
|---|---|---|---|---|

**Types of Movement and Change (syntax)**

add depth
augment
blur
build
color
contour
delete
dissolve
distort
drop shadow
enter-exit ——— •
fill with pattern
follow path
gradate
invert
make amorphous
mask
overlap
replace
reveal
rotate
shuffle
skew
soften
zoom

**Museum Key Words (meaning)**

**Level 1**

*verbs:*
• clarify
• collect
• display
• discover
  integrate
• isolate
• peruse
  piece together
  preserve
  restore
• reveal
• select

*nouns:*
change
craft
decoration
• encounters
  growth
  life styles
• migration
• passages
  place: ———
• process
  source
• time line
  treasure
  values

*adjectives:*
contextual
• diverse
  old
• accessible

**Level 2**

farmstead reconstruction
prairie reconstruction
temporary exhibitions
permanent exhibition hall
log cabin in main hall: ———

**Level 3**

bed
cabinet
clock
cradle
cast-iron stove: ———
people (mannequins)
rocking chairs
rugs
spinning wheel
textiles
utensils
etc.

**Level 4**

sculptural spiral motif in flanges

universal themes

specific themes

The syntactic, or formal, change of entering and/or exiting the stage, to take one example, can be used to support many different ideas such as those marked with a dot under level 1.

(Each level yields new key words, as seen on the scores, pages 199–200.)

### Coupling Form and Meaning

The table compares formal operations stemming from the animation medium and the list of key words for the museum. What we expect is that the key words will help to suggest formal possibilities and serve as a criterion to evaluate formal action.

Connecting one kind of action (enter-exit) to words to which it might relate (clarify, collect, display, discover, isolate, peruse, and so on) shows that the application of form to meaning is not fully predictable. If it were, we would end up with stereotypes. Rather, the juxtaposition of the lists should suggest trying things out. *How* any concept is made to work is a matter of imagination. For imagination to be translated to reality it requires a feedback process. Key words give constant, concise feedback to help in keeping a statement focused without predetermining the outcome.

At the head of each score shown on pages 199-200, a short list of key words is coupled to the formal operations used in the score along with a summary description of the relationship of form and meaning.

| Effect ▼ | Symbol ▼ | Description and Modifier Range | Effect ▼ | Symbol ▼ | Description and Modifier Range |
|---|---|---|---|---|---|
| | | **amorphous** recognizable—not recognizable (e.g., here barely recognizable) | | | **invert** |
| | | **augment** describe augmentation | | | **mask** define image to be masked (e.g., cast-iron stove medallion) |
| | | **color** show actual color cycling instructions  *dark-light gradient*  *cycle through purples* | | | **pattern fill** dots—lines curved—straight very coarse—very fine (draw pattern increment) |
| | | **contour** complete—broken thick—thin | *waving grasses* | R | **real time fill** describe image and action mark centers |
| | | **delete** | | | **replace** define new part (e.g., here Garamond Alternate Italic *M*) |
| | | **depth (spatial): drop shadow solid** very shallow—very deep direction | | | **revert to home form** |
| | | **distort** friendly—destructive mild—severe | | | **skew** backward—forward define angle |
| | | **gradient (as a function of form, not motion)** subtle—contrasting direction of shift | | | **soften** even—uneven coarse—fine mild—severe blur |

**B. Movement**
**1. Sequence Motion**

**2. Custom changes**
**in position or arrangement**

| Effect ▼ | Symbol ▼ | Description and Modifier Range |
|---|---|---|
| | | **checkerboard build or dissolve**<br>small chunks—large chunks<br>very fast—very slow |
| | | **dot build or dissolve (random)**<br>very coarse—very fine<br>round—square particles<br>very fast—very slow |
| | | **line build or dissolve (blinds)**<br>horizontal—vertical<br>very fast—very slow |
| | | **line build or dissolve (random)**<br>horizontal—vertical<br>very fast—very slow |
| | | **size change**<br>large to small<br>small to large<br>minimum—maximum<br>abrupt or zoom<br>(e.g., maximum large to small zoom) |
| | | **wipe**<br>reveal or remove<br>very fast—very slow<br>direction<br>smooth or stepped |

| Effect ▼ | Symbol ▼ | Description and Modifier Range |
|---|---|---|
| | | **enter stage**<br>**exit stage**<br>**cross stage**<br>direction<br>very slow—very fast |
| | | **follows path**<br>(show desired path shape) |
| | | **overlap, opaque**<br>front and back or layer<br>numbers if more than two<br>**overlap, transparent** |
| | | **rotate (flat)**<br>clockwise—counterclockwise<br>very slow—very fast |
| | | **rotate (spatial)**<br>clockwise—counterclockwise<br>angle of tilt<br>very slow—very fast |
| | | **shuffle, systematic**<br>(e.g., on x axis only) |
| | | **shuffle, random**<br>(e.g., at random angles) |

| Operation | Notation | Explanation | Effect ▼ |
|---|---|---|---|

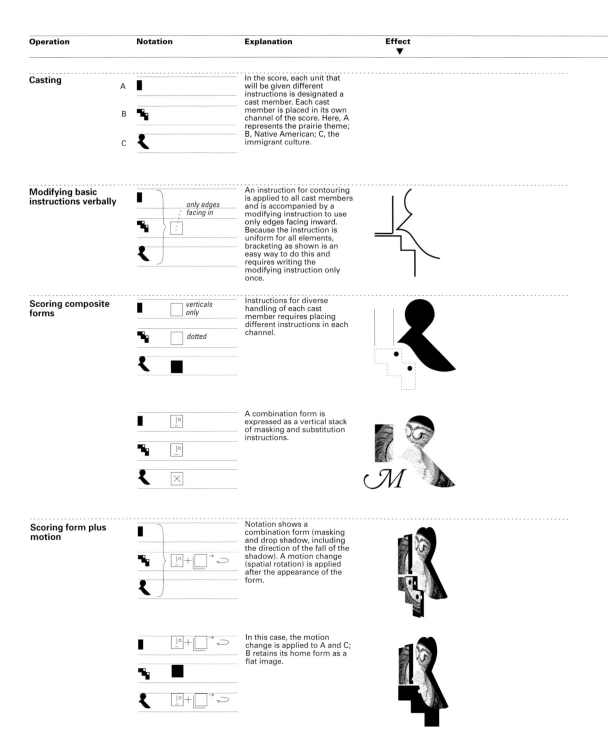

**Casting**

A ▪

B ▪▗

C ✆

In the score, each unit that will be given different instructions is designated a cast member. Each cast member is placed in its own channel of the score. Here, A represents the prairie theme; B, Native American; C, the immigrant culture.

**Modifying basic instructions verbally**

*only edges facing in*

An instruction for contouring is applied to all cast members and is accompanied by a modifying instruction to use only edges facing inward. Because the instruction is uniform for all elements, bracketing as shown is an easy way to do this and requires writing the modifying instruction only once.

**Scoring composite forms**

*verticals only*

*dotted*

Instructions for diverse handling of each cast member requires placing different instructions in each channel.

A combination form is expressed as a vertical stack of masking and substitution instructions.

**Scoring form plus motion**

Notation shows a combination form (masking and drop shadow, including the direction of the fall of the shadow). A motion change (spatial rotation) is applied after the appearance of the form.

In this case, the motion change is applied to A and C; B retains its home form as a flat image.

---

## Scoring text

Kauffman Museum

K    auffman    M    useum

In general, text is treated as any other cast member. Here the initial *K* enters from the left, the rest of the word builds randomly. The initial *M* appears from the left; the rest of the word builds with a reveal from the top.

In many cases, as shown here, the number of channels can be reduced by breaking up the text and placing the relevant text parts below the symbols.

| Operation | Notation | Explanation |
|---|---|---|

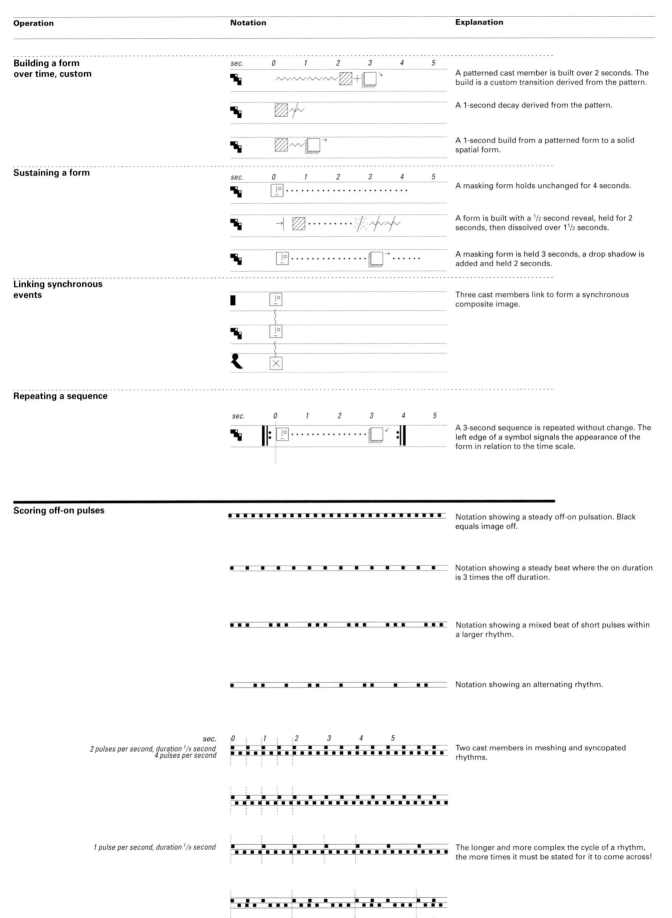

**Building a form over time, custom**

A patterned cast member is built over 2 seconds. The build is a custom transition derived from the pattern.

A 1-second decay derived from the pattern.

A 1-second build from a patterned form to a solid spatial form.

**Sustaining a form**

A masking form holds unchanged for 4 seconds.

A form is built with a ½ second reveal, held for 2 seconds, then dissolved over 1½ seconds.

A masking form is held 3 seconds, a drop shadow is added and held 2 seconds.

**Linking synchronous events**

Three cast members link to form a synchronous composite image.

**Repeating a sequence**

A 3-second sequence is repeated without change. The left edge of a symbol signals the appearance of the form in relation to the time scale.

**Scoring off-on pulses**

Notation showing a steady off-on pulsation. Black equals image off.

Notation showing a steady beat where the on duration is 3 times the off duration.

Notation showing a mixed beat of short pulses within a larger rhythm.

Notation showing an alternating rhythm.

2 pulses per second, duration ⅛ second
4 pulses per second

Two cast members in meshing and syncopated rhythms.

1 pulse per second, duration ⅛ second

The longer and more complex the cycle of a rhythm, the more times it must be stated for it to come across!

**Process:**

**1**
*Define the basic concept.*

**2**
*Determine a time interval and duration.*

**3**
*Sketch cast members.*

**4**
*Determine their possible appearance order.*

**5**
*Sketch the cast member events in rough form.*

**6**
*Build the counterpoint events between cast members. The rough sketch may be adequate preparation for developing the cast and score in MMD.*

**7**
*Refine the score.*

**8**
*Convert the score to animation in MMD:*
*• Develop the actual visual character of the cast members by drawing or by importing images or by creating texts.*
*• Place cast members in the score window and assign transitions and color.*
*• Revise tempos, transitions, and color palettes to achieve the desired flow of events.*
*(The examples furnished on disk can be played without additional software. The actual casts and scores can be analyzed using the MacroMind Director® program.)*

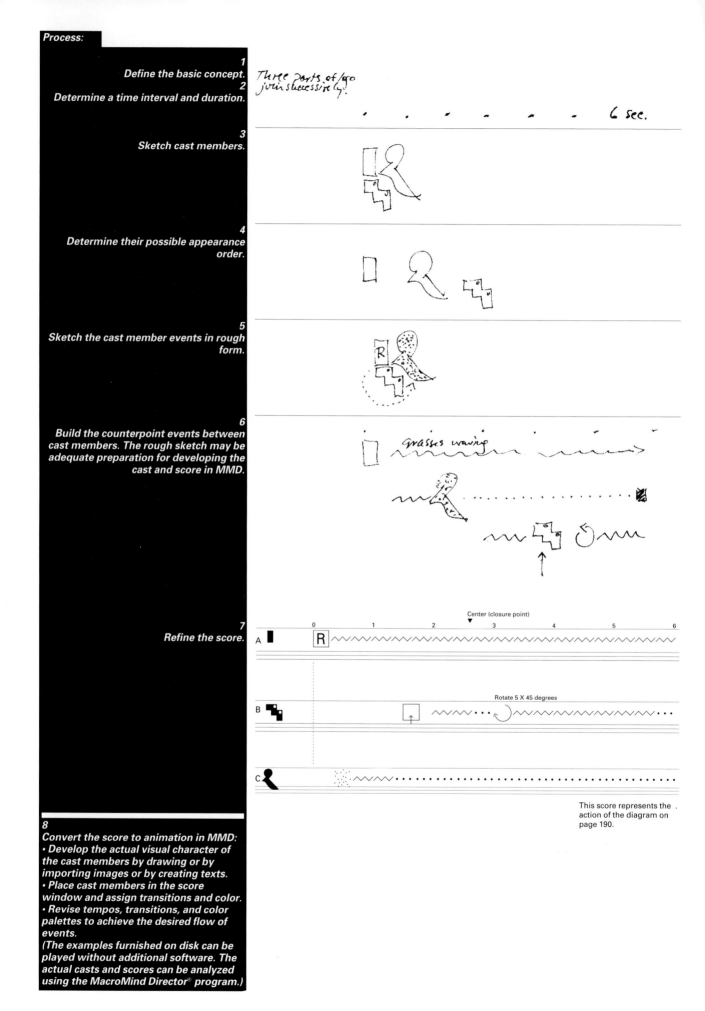

This score represents the action of the diagram on page 190.

## Sample Score 1:
## A score for two cast members to introduce the logo

*Form and meaning:*
Rotation of B plays on its dual role as an *M* form and completion of the *K*.

*Key words:*
integrate
*M* as part of *K*
putting things in context
ritual dances

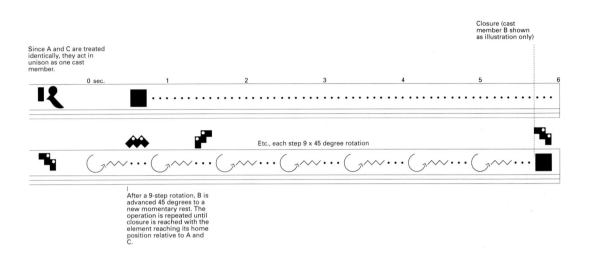

Closure (cast member B shown as illustration only)

Since A and C are treated identically, they act in unison as one cast member.

Etc., each step 9 x 45 degree rotation

After a 9-step rotation, B is advanced 45 degrees to a new momentary rest. The operation is repeated until closure is reached with the element reaching its home position relative to A and C.

## Sample Score 2:
## A score with three cast members and text

*Form and meaning:*
Logo is introduced in a sequence relating to the historical progression: prairie, native culture, immigrant culture.

*Key words:*
assemble
build
collect

ABC hold their home forms, then overlap (transparent).

Text enters in four stages and overlaps ABC (opaque). The layering sequence is indicated by numbers.

**A**

Off pulse
Color

A appears as a patterned form, then blinks in a 1:3 rhythm after which it dissolves to its home form over .5 second.

**B**

B builds as a solid dimensional form, blinks in a 1:1 rhythm synchronous with A and dissolves to its home form.

**C**

C enters the stage from right and dissolves to its home form.

**Text**

K   auffman   M   useum

All

**Stage**

Color

The entire stage is defined as a constant dark gray.

Closure occurs when the three cast members reveal the composite logo image. This is a center.

## Sample Score 3:
### A score for four cast members to couple the logo with a stationary visual image: detail from a cast-iron stove

*Form and meaning:*
Hot colors of the logo are progressively revealed using a standard stepped reveal. The forms come into partly concealed relationship to the stove image using transparency and layering. The stove symbolizes vitality and a high level of decorative craft.

*Key words:*
craft
decoration
heat
flame
durability
spiral

Composite stage drawing, home position

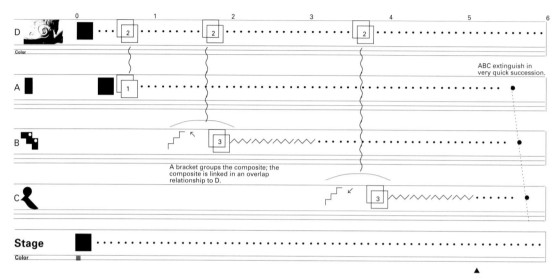

ABC extinguish in very quick succession.

A bracket groups the composite; the composite is linked in an overlap relationship to D.

▲
Closure occurs when C is fully revealed.

## Sample Score 4:
### A score for four cast members to couple the logo with an animated visual image: threshing stone

*Form and meaning:*
A coarse screen image of a threshing stone rotates continuously and slightly eccentrically to feel like it is grinding. The logo parts pop in successively. Their transparency makes the coarse grain and color of the stone image move inside the logo.
Diverse color palettes change mood from somber to joyous to festive depending on whether the connection will be to the work of threshing, to the celebration of harvest, or other connotations.

*Key words:*
turning
grinding
grain
simplicity

Composite stage drawing, home position

Repeats with color palette change for each loop.

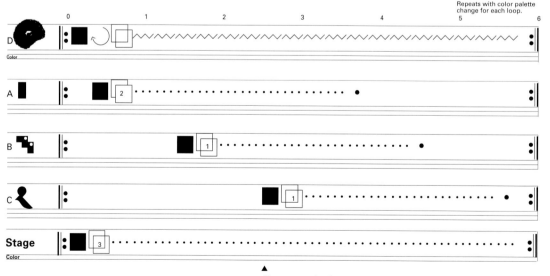

▲
Closure occurs when C appears.

## Summary of Notation Symbols

The symbols are essentially linear to allow easy notation by pencil or pen. This page may be duplicated as a work sheet.

### A. Changes in form

|  |  |
|---|---|
| ⌒ | amorphous |
| ⌂ | augment |
| ☰ | color |
| ▢ | contour |
| • | delete |
| | depth, shadow |
| | depth, solid |
| | distort |
| ‖‖ | gradient |
| ▮ | invert |
| | mask |
| ▨ | pattern fill |
| R | real time |
| ☒ | replace |
| ◼ | revert to home form |
| / | skew |
| ∫ | soften |

**composite examples:**

|  |  |
|---|---|
| | mask+solid |
| ⌒ | augment+amorphous |
| ▨ | distort+pattern |
| | etc. |

### B. Movement
### 1. Sequence Motion

|  |  |
|---|---|
| | checkerboard build |
| | checkerboard dissolve |
| ⋰ | dot build |
| ⋰ | dot dissolve |
| ☰ | line build |
| ≢ | line dissolve |
| | random line build |
| ≢ | random line dissolve |
| < | size change, abrupt |
| ⩻ | size change, zoom |
| →| | wipe, reveal |
| ⤳ | wipe, remove |
| ⌐ | wipe, stepped edge |
| ❋ | direction of motion |

### 2. Custom changes

|  |  |
|---|---|
| →| | cross stage |
| →| | enter stage |
| ↦ | exit stage |
| ⌣ | follows path |
| ■■ | off-on pulse |
| � | overlap, opaque |
| ▤ | overlap, transparent |
| ↻ | rotate |
| ↺ | |
| ↪ | rotate, spatial |
| ⬭ | |
| ⋰ | shuffle, random |
| ⋰ | shuffle, systematic |
| ❋ | direction of motion |

### C. Linking Symbols

|  |  |
|---|---|
| ⌇ | build over time |
| + | combine with |
| { | link cast members |
| ⋯ | sustain unchanged |
| ‖⁞‖ | repeat segment |

| 1 ............................ | Video:<br>Sony CCD-110V 8mm camera<br>MacVision® video digitizing software and<br>hardware |
|---|---|
| 2 ............................ | Sound:<br>MacRecorder® sound digitizer |
| 3 ............................ | Scanner:<br>Apple Scanner with Abaton 8-bit upgrade |
| 4 ............................ | Tape Back-up:<br>40 MB Jasmine DirectTape® |
| 5 ............................ | CPU:<br>Macintosh II computer with 8 MB RAM<br>13″ Applecolor® Monitor<br>105 MB Maxcess internal hard drive<br>105 MB Jasmine external hard drive<br>40 MB Relax Mobile 42® removable hard<br>drive |
| 6 ............................ | Macintosh Plus computer with 2 MB RAM<br>40 MB Ehman hard drive |
| 7 ............................ | Printer:<br>LaserWriter NT® |

**Software, version numbers at completion of project:**
(The software used in each chapter is detailed on the respective chapter title pages.)
Applescan®
Canvas® 2.1
Digital Darkroom® 1.1
Fontographer® 3.2
Freehand® 2.02 and 3.0
Hyperscan®
Illustrator 88® 1.6
MacroMind Director® 2.0
MacVision® 2.0
Microsoft Word® 4.0
Pagemaker® 4.01

**Utilities:**
Abaton Scan DA®
Big Thesaurus®
Capture®
DiskTop®
EZMenu®
QuicKeys®
SmartScrap®
Suitcase®
WordFinder®

**Type Faces:**
Adobe Univers and Garamond 3 families
Custom fonts for Chapter 5 and morphologies designed using Fontographer®

**Output specifications:**
Linotronic 330 film output @ 2540 dpi
by The Type Connection, Philadelphia

This book was produced at an Apple Macintosh work station. As the photograph shows, the equipment came to be organized in a circle configuration starting with a conventional drawing board that doubled as a small-scale video staging area, and ending with a laser printer. The magnifier-lamp on an extension arm proves to be a very versatile single light source for the video takes.

A scanner sits just to the left of the computer. Some of the work for this book was scanned at 4-bits (16 levels of gray) in Applescan and Hyperscan. An upgrade to 8-bits (256 levels of gray) allowed better gray-scale range. However, many interesting custom screen effects are possible with low resolution equipment.

The monitor/keyboard set-up allows for the hands to be lower than the elbow, important to avoid repetitive motion syndrome. The monitor screen is more than arm's length from the eyes, both to diminish the effect of magnetic radiation and, as described on page 20, to allow for global viewing of the screen image. As a further advantage, a drawer for the keyboard also frees up a work space between the keyboard and the monitor. With an extension copyholder, the hard copy being keyboarded can be brought closer to you than to the screen. PageMaker's "story" mode lets you view text in large scale while maintaining distance from the computer screen. In my case, I chose a 14 point serif face (a serif face so I could see if ligatures had been converted).

To work experimentally with combinations of imagery in Multifinder, 8 Megabytes (MB) of RAM were required. For example, in the final chapter on graphics in motion, I had Freehand open to produce the drawings for the morphology and the score samples, Fontographer open to work on the font developed for the symbols, and PageMaker open to receive the changes and integrate them. This multi-tasking environment allows the design of a component to be immediately integrated, tested, and revised. For the management of files (including their moving, copying, and naming) while programs are open, I cannot say enough in praise of DiskTop. EZMenu allows scanning of menus without finger pressure on the mouse, a very significant help in relieving muscle tension in long sessions.

On-line storage memory is 200 MB, 100 MB each in an internal and external drive. Even with this amount of memory it was never possible to have the whole book on the hard disks. Most chapters accumulated to consist of 20-40MB including banks of alternate drawings or other images. So at the end, no more than two or three chapters would be in hard disk memory, since I was also maintaining large system, application, and client files. Finally, a 40 MB Syquest removable drive was added to facilitate the transmission of documents for Linotronic output.

Back-up storage was on 40 MB tapes, with a second, complete set of current back-ups in a remote location for security.

Originally, I budgeted a 19" gray scale monitor; however, memory requirements took precedence over monitor convenience. Fortunately, PageMaker's Story Editor permits text editing at a larger size with page layout in reduced size mode.

The growth of the system was evolutionary, and in the course of adjusting its size and extent to my needs, I experienced the usual problems in compatibility, termination on the SCSI bus, etc. Three hard disks failed during this time; some data was lost. Some projects improved in the reconstruction, some definitely suffered. Manufacturers accused each other of not following Apple's protocol. Manuals were inexcusably complex. Often I had to write my own "quick reference" summaries to clarify a procedure. But that's the best way to learn. Some of my training in dealing with the system and hardware aspects of the computer came through telephone sessions, being "walked through" procedures by technical support personnel of software and hardware vendors in order to overcome problems or save data. I found these technicians to be exceedingly patient. The magazines of the trade helped, although they have grown to be excessive behemoths from both a functional and visual standpoint.

A modem port switcher let me shift among the peripherals using the same serial port: video and sound digitizers, and the modem itself. The computer and adjacent peripherals plug into a commonly grounded controller with individually surge-protected circuits.

A MacPlus, my original Macintosh and next in the circle, was frequently used to produce text or drawing files while the MacII was tied up in long printing times. Originally, during the RAM scarcity, having a second computer with a different program open served as an ad hoc "multifinder."

The equipment circle is completed with a LaserWriter NT. Since the fonts used all require downloading, printing was more tedious than would have been the case with a printer with more memory for more resident fonts. The output is at arm's length behind the computer, and the ozone exhaust from the printer is directed away from it.

All of the pages were produced in single, integrated pages on film, without additional stripping, except for the color separations in chapter 6. These were scanned, separated, and stripped in.

One of the greatest dilemmas in working with this process is the discrepancy between laser and imagesetter outputs. Remakes of about 5 percent of the pages were required to clear up these problems. Some discrepancies remain!

The book was begun in the fall of 1988 and completed in May, 1991. In two and a half years, the programs used for drawing and layout underwent major upgrades, each bringing the attendant benefits and complications. Enhancements to PageMaker, including the Story Editor, the index creation tools, and link manager came just in time to be useful in the final production of the book.

A specialized bibliography for graphic design exists elsewhere. Design as a process, however, is the synthesis of knowledge and information from many sources. Thus I have often chosen to quote from sources that come from perspectives outside of graphic design *per se,* and that seemed appropriate to make a point. These are not necessarily recommended readings; rather, like this book in general, they suggest that the experienced assimilation of information is part of anyone's process toward uniqueness.

Sources are listed in order of appearance.

**page 3**

Le Corbusier, *Creation is a Patient Search.* New York: Praeger, 1960. L-C titled his book in reference to both his own incessant search to understand modern building materials and forms, and also to the time it takes industry to put in practice the creativity of architects. Patience is essential to process but discovery is the reason for it.

**page 7**

Whitehead, Alfred North. *The Aims of Education.* New York: The Free Press, 1957.

**Introduction**

Weingart, Wolfgang. *Octavo 87.4.* Octavo: London, 1987. Weingart discusses his educational approach in a profusely illustrated lecture "How Can One Make Swiss Typography?"

Maki, Fumihoko. In "Japan's master architect shares blueprint for success" by Thomas Hine, *The Philadelphia Inquirer,* 5 June 1990.

Bruner, Jerome. *The Process of Education.* Cambridge: Harvard University Press, 1960.

Blake, William is quoted in *The Engineer of Human Souls* by Josef Svorecki. Washington Square Press: New York, 1977. p. xi.

France, Anatole, also quoted in Svorecki, p. xi.

Whitehead, Alfred North. *The Aims of Education.* New York: The Free Press, 1957. p. 31.

Bach, Johann Sebastian, quoted in: D.V.T. Khan. *Introducing Spirituality into Counseling and Therapy,* Lebanon Springs: Omega Press, 1982. Copyright by the Sufi Order.

Williams, William Carlos. From "The Orchestra." In *Pictures from Brueghel and Other Poems.* New York: New Directions Books, 1962.

Wolpe, Stefan. "Lecture on Dada." *Musical Quarterly* vol. 72, no. 2, 1986. p 205. The composers extemporaneous remarks from a remarkable lecture in 1962 speak poetically of the simultaneity of experience.

Bateson, Gregory. *Mind and Nature.* Toronto: Bantam Books, 1979.

Dörr, Alfred. *Komponisten des 20. Jahrhunderts in der Paul Sacher Stiftung.* Basel: Kunstmuseum, 1986. p. 23.

Anonymous Eskimo. From an exhibition "Innuit Games: Traditional Sport and Play of the Eskimo," organized by the Arts and Learning Services Foundation, Minneapolis, 1989.

Goldberger, Paul. "Within Limits." *New York Times Magazine,* 7 April 1991.

Lupton, Ellen, and Miller, J. Abbott, editors. *the abc's of ▲■●, the bauhaus and design theory.* Writing/Culture Monograph V. The Herb Lubalin Study Center of Design and typography. New York: The Cooper Union, 1991. This monograph contains an excellent summary of the Froebel method.

Pagels, Elaine. *The Gnostic Gospels.* New York: Random House, 1979. Pagels gives an enlightening account of the suppression of mysticism and individualism by paternalistic church fathers.

Blum, David. "A Process Larger Than Oneself." *The New Yorker.* May 1989. This profile of the cellist Yo-Yo Ma is a refreshing and lively expression of the process of artistic growth.

Frankl, Viktor E. *Man's Search for Meaning.* New York: Washington Square Press, 1963.

Alexander, Christopher. *Notes on the Synthesis of Form.* Cambridge: Harvard University Press, 1967.

Alexander, Christopher. "A City is not a Tree," *Design.* London, 1966. This essay has occasionally been revised and appears also in *Design after Modernism,* ed. by John Thackera. New York: Thames and Hudson, 1988.

Piaget, Jean. *Structuralism.* New York: Harper and Row, copyright 1970 by Basic Books.

Le Corbusier. *The Radiant City.* New York: Orion, 1967. L-C develops the argument for plan and planning in relation to machine-age specialization.

Lévi-Strauss. *The Raw and the Cooked.* New York: Harper and Row, 1969.

Benjamin, Walter. From "The Rigorous Study of Art" in *October 47.* Cambridge: MIT Press, Winter, 1988.

Eco, Umberto. *Foucault's Pendulum.* New York: Harcourt Brace Jovanovitch, 1989.

Berry, Wendell. *Home Economics.* Berkeley: North Point Press, 1988.

Zukaw, Gary. *The Dancing Wu Li Masters.* Bantam Books, 1980.

Campbell, Jeremy. *Grammatical Man.* New York: Simon and Shuster, 1982. p. 105.

Lévi-Strauss, Claude. *Structural Anthropology.* Garden City: Anchor Books, 1967.

d'Arcy Thompson, Wentworth. Quoted in Alexander, *Notes,* op.cit. p. 15.

Campbell, Jeremy. op. cit. pp. 127, 164, 173–74.

Campbell, Joseph. *The Power of Myth,* with Bill Moyers. New York: Doubleday, 1988.

Malle, Louis. Quoted from an interview on "Fresh Air" by Terry Gross, produced by WHYY, Philadelphia. Distributed on National Public Radio. This and other quotations from interviews on WHYY used by permission. "Fresh Air" has for years been a welcome late afternoon relief, a time when creativity seems to run dry—a time for receptivity.

Yourçenar, Margaret. *The Memoirs of Hadrian.* Hamondsworth: Penguin Books, 1978.

Woolman, John. *The Journal and Major Essays of John Woolman,* edited by Philip Moulton. New York: Oxford University Press, 1971.

Valenti, Benita. As quoted from "Fresh Air."

Gleizes, Albert and Metzinger, Jean. "Cubism" In *Modern Artists on Art: Ten Unabridged Essays,* edited by Robert L. Herbert. Englewood Cliffs: Prentice-Hall, 1964.

Holan, Vladimir. In Svorecki. p. 365.

Beckett, Samuel. *Watt.* New York: Grove Press, 1970.

Pound, Ezra. "Speech and Writing in Poetry and Its Criticism." *Visible*

*Language* vol. xxii, no. 2/3. Providence: Spring 1988.

Taylor, John F. A. *Design and Expression in the Visual Arts*. New York: Dover, 1964.

Barzun, Jacques. From "A Little Matter of Sense." In *The New York Times,* 21 June 1990.

Eco, Umberto. op. cit. p. 255.

Cocteau, Jean. Quoted in chapter on "Growth" in *Art and Visual Perception* by Rudolf Arnheim. Berkeley: University of California Press, 1974. While creativity is generally marked by crossing boundaries, most great artists and designers show an organic growth process that builds progressively.

Gillespie, Dizzy. Quoted from the *Horizon Series* on public radio station WHYY, Philadelphia.

Campbell, Jeremy. op. cit. p. 144.

Rand, Paul. *Paul Rand: A Designer's Art*. New Haven: Yale University Press, 1985. Though I have not quoted Paul Rand, I would be remiss not to acknowledge my debt to him. Rand exemplifies the visual thinking person, able to strip away burdensome affectation. In a long life of youthful exuberance in design, Rand was a hero of my youth and continues through the six-fold renewal of my body cells to be a force and inspiration.

## Chapter 1

Kandinsky, Wassily. *Point and Line to Plane*. New York: Dover, 1979.

Hofmann, Armin. *Graphic Design Manual*. New York: Van Nostrand Reinhold, 1965. This volume deals with fundamental questions in design, each example is worked out through an intensive finding process by Hofmann's students from the period during which the author attended Hofmann's courses. See *Armin Hofmann: His Works, Quest and Philosophy* (Basel: Birkhauser, 1990) for an exposition of Hofmann's own work in a wide range of applications, especially sign-symbols, posters, and architectural graphics.

Wolfert, Paula. *Mediterranean Cooking*. New York: Times Books, 1977.

Anderson, Laurie. *IT Tango,* copyright 1982 by Difficult Music.

Calvino, Italo. *Invisible Cities*. New York: Harcourt Brace Jovanovitch, 1974.

de Saussure, Ferdinand. *Cours de Linguistique Generale*. Lausanne: Bally

and Sechehaye, 1916.

Mallarmé, Stéphane. *A Tomb for Anatole*. Translated by Paul Auster. Berkeley: North Point Press, 1983.

Ghyka, Matila. *The Geometry of Art and Life*. New York: Dover, 1977.

Thirring, Walter and Needham, Joseph. Quoted in *The Tao of Physics* by Fritjof Kapra. Toronto: Bantam, 1977.

## Chapter 2

Campbell, Jeremy. op. cit. p. 160.

Bruner, Jerome. *The Process of Education*. Cambridge: Harvard University Press, 1960.

The morphology of letter form is adapted and applied from a morphology developed by Karl Gerstner in *Compendium for Literates*. Cambridge: MIT Press, 1974. Gerstner's earlier contribution to systematic thinking in *Designing Programmes* (New York: Hastings House, 1968) was a significant one, however, it is now out of print.

Levinson, D.H. "What business can do for schools." *The Philadelphia Inquirer*, 10 December, 1989. Levinson quotes Edison on the search/research process.

Fowles, John. *The Enigma of Stonehenge*. Photographs by Barry Brukoff. New York: Summit Books, copyright 1980 by The Philpot Museum.

## Chapter 4

Waldman, Diane. *Mark Rothko, 1903-1970: A Retrospective*. New York: Guggenheim/Abrams, 1978.

Justema, William. *Pattern: A Historical Panorama*. Boston: New York Graphic Society, 1976.

Barthes, Roland. *The Responsibility of Forms*. New York: Hill and Wang, 1985. Translation, copyright 1985 by Farrar, Straus and Giroux, Inc.

Blum, David. I have seen Yo-Yo Ma perform as a soloist, then join the orchestra cello section (the last row!) for a pure orchestral work, a chance for him to learn more. Seeing him in person and in TV interviews, Yo-Yo Ma impresses you as the consummate performer and ever-humble learner-seeker.

Rohrer, Warren. From a personal conversation, 1989. I first referred to Rohrer's work as "color field" paintings. He said

he thinks of them more as "fields of color."

Thoreau, Henry David. *In Wildness is the Preservation of the World*. New York: Sierra Club, 1962.

Gerstner, Karl. *The Forms of Color*. Noted separately under Chapter 5, this volume includes a notable section on Islamic geometric pictures.

## Chapter 5

Birren, Faber. *Principles of Color*. New York: Van Nostrand Reinhold, 1969. A simplified statement of the rules of color as compiled from the work of Birren and others.

Kueppers, Harald. *The Basic Law of Color Theory*. Woodbury: Barron's, 1982. An excellent, scientifically-based exposition, especially of laws of color mixing.

Albers, Josef. *The Interaction of Color*. New Haven: Yale University Press, 1963. A poetic chronicle of the work of an outstanding educator in discovering principles at work in an illusory world.

. . . . .

In addition to the above, the following make significant contributions to the understanding of color:

Chevreul, M.E. *The Principles of Harmony and Contrast of Colors*. New York: Van Nostrand Reinhold, 1967. Especially cogent observations on simultaneous contrast and the effect of colors on each other by the Director of Dyes for the famous Gobelins tapestry works.

Friel, Edward. *The Friel System, a language of color*. Seattle: Edward Friel, 1961. An esoteric approach to the diagramming of color based on typical pigments used by painters.

Gerritsen, Frans. *Theory and Practice of Color*. New York: Van Nostrand Reinhold, 1975. A good display of color diagrams through history.

Gerstner, Karl. *The Spirit of Color*. Cambridge: MIT Press, 1981. Essays and projects from the vantage point of a free-spirited constructivist, excellently printed.

———. *The Forms of Color*. Cambridge: MIT Press, 1986. A brilliant digest of form systems, including Günter Wysecki's *uniform color space*.

Itten, Johannes. *The Art of Color*. New York: Van Nostrand Reinhold Company, 1961. The subjective experience and objective rationale of color.

Jacobson, Egbert. *Basic Color, An Interpretation of the Ostwald Color System.* Chicago: Paul Theobald, 1948. Extensive and refined application of color harmonics based on geometries found within the color sphere, excellently diagrammed.

Klee, Paul. *The Thinking Eye: note books.* ("Documents of Modern Art," vol. 15.) Edited by Jürg Spiller. Translated by Ralph Manheim. New York: Wittenborn, 1961. Projects for the understanding of color in cosmic terms. The definition of the basic color structure as a sphere in *Graphic Design Processes* traces in part to Klee's placement of color in a spherical form, which behaves nicely as an archetype and less well as a scientific structure. (See Gerstner's presentation of Wysecki in *The Forms of Color*, above.)

Stockton, James. *A Designer's Guide to Color.* San Francisco: Chronicle Books, 1984. A reference tool for examining specific color combinations.

**Chapter 6**

Payzant, Geoffrey. *Glenn Gould, Music and Mind.* Toronto: Key Porter Books, 1984. Payzant explains Gould's welcoming of the electronic age: "Each person must accept the challenge of contemplatively creating his own 'divinity.' 'Divinity' here refers to the better part of individual human nature, which for Gould is the introspectively and ecstatically contemplative part; the worse part is that which abandons itself to herd impulse, as in the mindless, hysterical response of crowds to spectacles and of populations to propaganda. In 1974 Gould wrote: 'I believe in the intrusion of technology because, essentially, that intrusion imposes upon art a notion of morality which transcends the idea of art itself....' From Gould's context it would seem that the destructiveness of art is in its competitive aspects, and 'the areas where it tends to do least harm' are those areas in which the adrenal factor is mitigated by technology."

Wolpe, Stefan. "Lecture on Dada." *Musical Quarterly* vol. 72, no. 2, 1986. p 203.

Fenellon, Ernest. "The Chinese Written Character as a Medium for Poetry." In *Prose Keys to Modern Poetry*, edited by Karl Shapiro. New York: Harper and Row, 1962.

**Chapter 7**

Dörr, Alfred. *Komponisten des 20. Jahrhunderts in der Paul Sacher Stiftung.* Basel: Kunstmuseum, 1986. Feldman's score for *Sequenza III* breaks from conventional notation in many respects, but maintains the traditional left-right, top-down reading order. For more visual and spatial scores, see *Notations*, compiled by John Cage. New York: Something Else Press, 1969.

Zettl, Herbert. *Sight, Sound, Motion.* Belmont, CA: Wadsworth, 1973. A comprehensive introduction to design and production of film and television.

von Arx, Peter. *Film Design.* New York: Van Nostrand Reinhold, 1983. Peter von Arx's book is replete with brilliant examples of frame-by-frame development of graphic images. It is of inordinate value if only on the basis of the still graphic images developed by graduate students at the School of Design in Basel, Switzerland.

**All photographs are by the author unless
otherwise credited. Photo on the back
cover is by Bennett Lorber.**